ENCOURAGEMENTS TOWARDS AWAKENING IN DAILY LIFE

BHANTE BODHIDHAMMA

A Satipanya Publication
Satipanya Buddhist Retreat White Grit Minsterley Shropshire
SY5 0JN www.satipanya.org.uk
Copyright© John Ridley 2020 All Rights Reserved
All royalties go to the work of Satipanya Buddhist Trust
Photograph of Satipanya Buddhist Retreat
Interior Book Design and Typesetting by FormatNow
International www.FormatNow.com

DEDICATION

None of these Tips would have been possible without Satipanya Retreat.

Whatever Goodness Power (puñña) is accrued through this work,
may it be to the benefit of all those
who by little or large offerings of time and wealth
have contributed to the establishment of Satipanya.

PREFACE

Once Satipanya started running retreats in July 2007, newsletters took on a greater importance. At first, we had to post all our 'Newsbytes' to over a thousand people. Then in 2011, we went email. What a saving on post!

The main purpose was to advertise the courses, but also to keep people in touch with what was happening at the centre. I also felt there was a need for some Dhamma and so I started 'Tips o' the Day'. I am now assisted by Noirin Sheahan and Carl Fooks who both teach at the centre.

During this whole time, I have been indebted to Noirin as my chief editor, not so much literary as Dhammically, pointing to any lack of clarity and adding suggestions.

To get the script ready for publication, I was again given selfless service by Therese Caherty who brought a touch of professionalism into the work. And there was feedback from readers too that helped clarify points and support my efforts.

This is a collection of the last 12 years. The Tips were written without any overall plan. Sometimes they were topical, other times answering suggestions and mostly whatever I was interested to write about that month. Eventually when it came to publication, they seem to fit into various categories – Work, Wholesome and Unwholesome Qualities, Happiness, Relationship and Sundry Reflections and a detailed guide to meditation in daily life - none of them, of course, exhaustive.

As a companion to Encouragements to Awakening on Retreat, I decided to rename the Tips Encouragements to Awakening in Daily Life.

They are all around 500 words and meant as small reflections to excite further thought. They are by no means definitive statements. In fact, many topics have whole books written on them.

Necessarily all delusive thinking belongs to me and I ask the reader to exercise generosity of spirit.

Bhante Bodhidhamma
March 2020

CONTENTS

DAILY LIFE PRACTICE 12

    1. AT THE END OF THE DAY 13

    2. UPON AWAKENING 17

    3. PREPARING FOR TODAY 19

    4. DEVELOPING THE PERFECTION OF DETERMINATION ... 30

    5. BREAKFAST AT LAST! 32

    6. TRAVELLING TO AND FROM WORK 34

    7. BACK HOME 36

WORK 38

    1. WORK 39

    2. SUCCESS AND FAILURE : TRIAL AND ERROR 41

    3. CREATING SPACE – ENERGY 43

    4. CREATING SPACE –EMOTIONS 46

    5. CREATING SPACE – ATTENTION 48

    6. LIMITS OF POWER AND MISSION CREEP 50

SOME WHOLESOME AND SOME UNWHOLESOME QUALITIES 52

1. THE TOUGH NUT 53
2. IMPULSIVE OR SPONTANEOUS? 55
3. JOY! 57
4. THANK YOU 59
5. NEED SUFFICIENCY GREED 61
6. DIGNITY 63
7. PITY SORROW COMPASSION 65
8. SUBLIMATION 67
9. RIGHTEOUS ANGER : PLAIN ANGER 69
10. DISCIPLINE : SELF-DISCIPLINE 71
11. UNFORGIVINGNESS 74
12. THE CONSUMER IN US ALL 76
13. ISOLATION LONELINESS SOLITUDE 78
14. ENVY JEALOUSY APPRECIATIVE JOY 80
15. AWARENESS COMPASSION WISDOM 82
16. APPAMĀDA : DILIGENT 84
17. PASSIVE AGGRESSION 86
18. RIGHT SPEECH 89
19. EQUANIMITY 91
20. SHAME 93

21. GUILT 95

22. GRATITUDE GENEROSITY RENUNCIATION 97

23. EXCITEMENT BOREDOM CONTENTMENT 99

24. COURAGE FORTITUDE RESILIENCE 101

25. ONE OF THE HINDRANCES IS SCEPTICAL DOUBT 103

26. FEAR 105

27. PATIENCE 107

28. JUDGMENTAL OR JUDICIOUS? 109

29. OVERCOMING THE DISTORTIONS OF GENEROSITY 111

30. WHAT VALUES GOVERN OUR LIVES? 113

31. VALUES IN MINE OWN EYES 115

SEEKING TRUE HAPPINESS 117

1. NOT AN EMOTION 118

2. RELATIONSHIPS 120

3. BEING GOOD VERSUS BEING GOOD AT 122

4. WHAT'S WRONG WITH A BIT OF ATTACHMENT? 124

5. SACRIFICE: THE MORE WE GIVE THE GREATER THE RETURN 126

6. HOW WE LIVE, NOT WHAT WE BELIEVE 128

7. TOWARDS THE GREATEST HAPPINESS 130

RELATIONSHIPS 132

1. CULTIVATING PATIENCE: 133
2. FOUNTAINS OF JOY: 135
3. INTIMATE RELATIONSHIPS: EROTIC AND ROMANTIC LOVE 137
4. CELIBACY 139
5. WHEN DOES LOVE BECOME CONTROL? 141

SUNDRY REFLECTIONS 143

1. A NEW YEAR RESOLUTION 144
2. NEIGHBOURLY 'SOUNDS' 147
3. SICKNESS 149
4. LIVING IN THE NOW : PLANNING FOR THE FUTURE 151
5. MUSIC 153
6. TIME 155
7. TEA OR NIBBANA? 157
8. ON THE VIRTUE OF VISITING A CEMETERY 159
9. A PET'S ENDGAME PRELIMINARY THOUGHTS 161
10. MY BODY IS MOTHER EARTH 163
11. THE ABSURD AND THE SUBLIME : A MIDSUMMER CONTEMPLATION 165

12. IF THERE IS NO SELF, WHO BEARS THE KARMA? 168

13. OVERWHELMED BY ALL THE VIOLENCE IN THE WORLD? 170

14. LEGAL, MORAL, ETHICAL 172

15. BARRIERS OR BOUNDARIES? 174

16. UNWHOLESOME KARMIC RESULTS AS FATE 176

17. IDEOLOGY LEADS TO STRIFE 178

18. THE SACRED: ITS MEANING AND THE ROLE OF FREE SPEECH 181

19. AIM AND OBJECTIVE IN TIME PRESENT 184

20. IN WHAT WAY SHOULD BUDDHADHAMMA AFFECT OUR POLITICS? 186

21. PRACTICE MAKES PERFECT 189

22. SCIENTISM MEETS BUDDHISM (BUDDHADHAMMA) 191

23. OUR BASIC DISPOSITION TO LIFE 194

24. THE WISDOM OF UNCERTAINTY 197

25. WHY ARE WE ASKED TO OBSERVE ANICCA – IMPERMANENCE? 199

26. DEALING WITH INTENSE EMOTIONS AND MOODS IN ORDINARY DAILY LIFE 201

27. HOW MUCH PAIN, PHYSICAL OR MENTAL SHOULD WE SUFFER? 203

28. TO BECOME OR NOT TO BECOME 205

29. FAIRNESS AND EQUALITY 207

30. SILENCE 209

31. BEAUTY 211

32. DOWNERS 213

33. MONEY AND POWER 215

34. THE TREASURE OF THINGS 218

35. HUMOUR IS A FUNNY THING 220

36. PURPOSE IN LIFE 222

37. SATIPANYA BUDDHIST RETREAT 225

DAILY LIFE PRACTICE

1
AT THE END OF THE DAY

a) Preparing for Tomorrow

The next day begins the night before. How important it is to have a good night's sleep – and the deeper the sleep the more refreshed we feel. Sometimes we can wake up early feeling particularly bright, a sure sign that our sleep has been peaceful. How then to prepare for sleep?

The best practice is to stop all activity at least half an hour before we intend going to bed.

First, put the day to rest. Sitting quietly, let the day's events come to mind. It's best to do it systematically say from morn till night. As things that we don't feel too good about arise, put them right inwardly. Apologise where we feel we have harmed and forgive where we feel we have been harmed. Where we feel we have acted wholesomely, rejoice and determine to develop the underlying attitude even more. When others have been generous towards us, thank them.

As we pass each event, file it away, unless we wish to act on it – for instance apologise to or thank someone. Make a note if this is so.

Then let the general outlay of tomorrow come to mind – no need to be too specific. Consider briefly what our attitude and actions will be, for instance the attitude and manner we take to work. Then leave that on the back burner for the next day.

We may even think of writing it out as a dairy. Writing is useful here, more to stop thoughts wandering and to reflect constructively. It works even if we never read what we have written. This end of day reflection brings peace to the heart and matures our wisdom.

Once we have cleared this day and set ourselves at ease for the next one, we could do a little sitting, but at this time of night there is all the possibility of falling asleep. The evening sit is best done before dinner. If we do wish to sit, make it short and beware of the first signs of sleepiness. There is also metta, a more pro-active practice and therefore it's easier to stay awake during it. Or listen to music. Plain chant or Buddhist chanting is best because it comes out of silence and equanimity. It isn't emotional. Any music that promotes calmness will do. Don't forget there is poetry.

The overall objective is to rest all excitements and tribulations by stilling the body, quieting the mind and calming the heart.

b) Being in the moment

Spiritual practice demands that we make every moment absolutely important, not just because it is actually the only moment we have since past and future moments don't exist, but because it is only in the present moment that we can effect change.

How then to bring that sense of importance into everyday routine tasks, the ones we repeat often mindlessly. Preparing for bed is a prime example. The toiletry, the undressing, nestling into the mattress. Often done at speed to get it out of the way or the process hurled through by the longing for oblivion. Or in a sort of semi-consciousness, exhausted from the day's stresses, sleep walking into bed.

But we can make spiritual capital out of habitual ritual by turning it into something meaningful. By ritual I mean to imbue our actions with spiritual purpose.

Immediately, Right Mindfulness is brought to bear and with it Right Intention and so on to Right Action.

It's time to care for the body, to remind ourselves of its preciousness. Herein is housed the enlightened-being-to-be. It is through the body that this awakening will take place. So let's care for it. Let us appreciate it as our most valued vehicle. Let's treat it with the same reverence we give to our cars, our mobile phones and jewelry.

We have to bring the same attentiveness to those actions that we often care to disregard: to urinate and evacuate, Latinate words disguising our disgust. But good old, gritty Anglo-Saxon – piss and shit – often reveals our true relationship. How can we overcome such negativity to the body's natural and therefore neutral functions unless we attend to them? When we do this with the Right Intention – to care for the body – we see the role of tanha, that deluded distinction we make between pleasant and unpleasant where we indulge the one and crush the other. But there is a transcendent way to be with the pleasant and unpleasant and that is the equanimity we find in open acceptance – this is the way it is. And the joyful discovery is that the pleasant and the unpleasant still exist and they are okay.

Bring mindfulness to bear on the feel of things: Warm water on our hands and cheeks; the taste of the toothpaste; the comfort of the mattress.

Wash the face with the care a mother washes her baby. Brush the teeth as if we really treasure them, knowing how much we don't want dentures! Undress and dress for bed, treating our clothes as if they were the only ones we had. Lie on the snug mattress and for a moment bring to mind how lucky we are to live in such comparative luxury.

How many are the men, women and children this night with no soap but a stone, no clothes but rags, no bed but a pavement! Let us send them our metta.

c) Focus on the breath or metta

Finally, we are in bed about to enter a deep sleep. We've cleared a lot of the day's debris with an evening sitting, the metta practice and our end of day recollection. And we have prepared for bed mindfully and calmly.

So we are ready to 'disappear'. But even now memories, images and thinking can disturb us. They may be negative – sadnesses, irritations, anxieties. Or they may be positive – thinking around planning, achieving, romance. We must keep up that effort to be focused, yet relaxed. Occasionally the word concentration is used, but this I feel brings with it tension by its association with school or work. 'Focused' here means one-pointed, the thinking mind steadied on one object, the obvious one being the breath.

Again the breath may have become associated with striving in our meditation. But to develop the calmness for sleep we need to feel the breath solely to contact calm, neutral feelings. We need to cultivate a taste for the neutral, the unexciting and begin to see that this is our default position. Once it has been cultivated we can contact it easily throughout the day.

To help us do this we can recall a time or place where we have felt calm and peaceful: on a beach, in a park, in our garden. And then contacting the feeling of tranquility in the body we sense it in the gentleness of the breath. This is a way of developing samatha, serenity.

And then there is metta. For this practice, it is best to choose someone whom we feel grateful to with no or minimal bad feelings towards. If we find it easy, we can direct metta towards ourselves and then to all beings. Just keep cycling round the trio. Keep the phrases short and simple: 'May you be well and happy.' In this way we develop a mental state saturated with loving feelings. The Buddha pointed to good restful sleep as one of the benefits of metta practice.

Another way is to offer metta to the body. Start from the head and go down the body blessing all the parts. After we reach the toes, start again from the top of the head. Moving up the body can lift energy. Keep the blessing simple: 'May you be healthy and strong.' We may find this creates exquisite gentle feelings. The cellular life enjoys a good watering of metta. It can be powerful if we feel restless – then we should try a comfortable position and refuse to move as we scan the body with metta.

We sleep in one-and-three-quarter hour waves, passing through four levels. The first three-and-half-hours are the most important since it is here that we sleep at the deepest level. Most articles I've read seem to say seven or eight hours is enough. If we live meditative lives, this is quite sufficient and we may find ourselves sometimes waking completely refreshed after five or six hours.

Finally make a firm determination to wake after seven or eight hours. You may be surprised to find you wake up on time. Even so don't forget to put the alarm on!

2

UPON AWAKENING

An alarm clock is all well and good, but it is often a rude awakening. Consider how we wake up on holiday, when we don't bother with an alarm. In contrast, an alarm's blast creates a shockwave in the mind and heart and we wake into that reaction - hardly a good start to the day. If we can muffle or lower the alarm, or opt for one that rises gradually, that is the better way to rouse oneself.

So we awake into a mood. It may be pleasant, unpleasant or neutral. Neutral is a peaceful start to the day. If the mood is pleasant, it will grab an idea from the mind's library and create a reverie. It will do the same should the mood be unpleasant.

These opening moments offer us an immediate practice, but to make them work to our advantage, we must be alert upon awakening. If we have made that resolute resolution to wake with the bell, we'll do this. It may take practice, but is not difficult to develop. We centre this immediate wakefulness into the body with special attention to that area in the mid-chest where we distinguish our emotional life. On recognising the mood, we acknowledge it and practise vipassana. And as in sitting meditation, we become equally aware of our reaction.

Should we open our eyes to a peaceful state, rest there and acknowledge it, grateful for this gift. Develop a taste for it. See it as a default position and resolve to return to it as often as possible throughout the day.

Should it be a pleasant state – excitement about what the day holds, a flowering romance, a joyful memory – whatever its cause, beware being transported into the dream world. But do acknowledge the state. See the danger of make-believe and wait, if possible, until with attention, all cools into an inner glow. This is quiet joy without attachment and we make a resolution to maintain it.

Should the mood be unpleasant – depression, anxiety, anger –whatever its cause, we prevent it from hurling us into a mental maelstrom. So we acknowledge the state, its danger, how the mood uses the mind to wind itself up. Bury the attention into the feeling and wait at least until it begins to subside. This is how we remove the sting from these unpleasant states. Then we make a resolution to stop negativity holding sway.

A sitting position is best for this as it is so easy to slide into sleep. And here the snooze button comes into its own, not simply to remind us of time passing, nor to appease the base desire to exercise one's sloth. Instead, it's the very opposite: to guard us from such indulgence of dire consequence! Such is the noble duty of the snooze button.

3

PREPARING FOR TODAY

a) Morning Meditation

All my teachers emphasised morning meditation – the first sitting of the day. It became a regular practice for me from the very start as Zazen.

It is the moment we set the orientation we hope to maintain throughout the day. And to me it always seemed a little rushed and unprepared to just plonk myself in posture and start meditating. But as with all important moments we perform a ritual to put ourselves in the right mode. Even going to work, we have our preening to do, the last glance in the mirror. So it is with sitting practice.

We remind ourselves of the importance of what it is we are about to do, simply lighting a candle may suffice. As a symbol of the spiritual, the candle is possibly the best example. Its light symbolises the path of insight and wisdom; its heat, the path of love and devotion; the flickering flame, the path of virtuous action.

I recommend bowing. So difficult for us, this act of surrender, of yielding. The Dhamma is always going to ask us to do what we (those self-serving selves) don't want to do. It is the body's language for 'I shall follow the teachings'. If you find this too bruising (the self always tells us it is silly, pointless –'I don't do bowing. If I bowed, it wouldn't be me.'), we may find it useful to bow inwardly and find for ourselves a phrase expressing desire to follow the Path.

If you get this far, you may even want to take the Refuges and Precepts. (download both chant and literature at www.satipanya.co.uk.) We have to make sense of these practices for ourselves. Taking Refuge in the Buddha traditionally is the historical personage, putting out trust (not blind faith) in the teacher, but it is also having confidence in the Buddha Within – that which seeks liberation. Taking Refuge in the Dhamma is traditionally the Buddha's teachings, but in this post-modern era we may wish to include all the teachings we find useful. And taking Refuge in the Sangha is again traditionally only those who have entered one of the Four Paths and Fruits and intuited Nibbana. For them all doubt as to the truth of the Buddha's teachings has gone. But given the importance his teachings put on good companionship, we may wish to include all our spiritual companions because their confidence and practice are great supports to us. Finally the Precepts are simply the basic training rules of the spiritual life.

We have to prepare ourselves mentally for important tasks. So find a way to help overcome any negativity or unwillingness to do the practice.

b) Abiding in calm open attentiveness

After performing a ritual, small or otherwise, with this Right Attitude developed to enter into the meditation we need now to establish Right Awareness.

When we look at the Seven Factors that Lead to Awakening, we see that awareness sits alone, but is supported by three passive and three active factors that pair each other: calmness with interest, effort with concentration and equanimity with investigation of the Dhamma.

In the Discourse on How to Establish Right Awareness, the Buddha starts by asking us to observe the breath in a gross way, to use it to calm ourselves and then to turn on the curiosity and observe the characteristic of impermanence.

The following exercise develops the passive qualities. It's best done standing, though we can change it to suit a sitting posture.

We feel the sensations in our feet and how they are changing. Slowly we move up the body, inside and on the surface, and continue to sense what is there. Once at the top of the head, feel sensations that arise on the scalp.

Now, turn the attention outward to hear sounds, see colours, sense the atmosphere of the room and so on. Once that outward awareness is established, bring into it the feelings in the feet, the breath and so on. In this way a spacious awareness is developed that softens the boundary between inside and outside.

Our attitude, meanwhile, is to develop calmness of the body and mind by relaxing in the posture; a steady attention (the noting is very helpful) which is our concentration; and receptivity. That's 'equanimity'. It means we are coming from a place of 'don't know' or 'not sure' and so stops concepts and opinions from distorting our experience and from an open-heart which prevents greed, aversion, fear, prejudice and preference.

Once this is established we can repeat to ourselves: Achieving nothing. (To achieve means we are always doing something now for some future result. But here we are just standing. Standing for standing's sake.) Going nowhere: Since we are totally in the present moment, we are right here – no planning needed. Being nobody: Since we are in silence and only in receptive mode, we don't have to perform, become a personality – no hope of celebrity here!

Once this open awareness with the attributes of calmness, the effort needed to support attentiveness, and equanimity as the default position within, we can switch on the curiosity and begin to investigate the Three Characteristics of Existence: Impermanence, Unsatisfactoriness and Not-self.

We can return to this mode at any time, but if we keep dropping into this default position throughout the day, we'll see the benefits.

c) Vipassana – developing a steady attention

Why is it so important to sit in the morning before we start 'doing'? It is simply because when we sit in vipassana we enter into a more sensitive level of awareness. We find ourselves in a relationship to the world that is different to the one that emerges from a non-vipassana awareness.

We know from our own practice that different principles and attitudes come into play when we develop this level of consciousness. And just in case we then feel superior, we remind ourselves that even when we are sitting, we rarely keep this up, never mind during daily life. More often than not we slip back down into greed, hatred and delusion. In fact, only a fully liberated person could maintain an unbroken vipassana awareness.

That said, our sit should begin with a firm resolute determination to establish right awareness. Using the noting, a deliberate noting, to keep the intellect tethered to the object, we place the attention on the feelings caused by the rise and fall of the abdomen. (Should you feel the breath at another place, please adjust these directions accordingly.)

The easiest way to establish a steady attention is to centre on the subtle, pleasant, neutral sensations, to taste their gentleness and to notice how the gentle rhythm calms the mind. Acknowledge this soft breath and calm mind as a resting place, a peaceful place. It sometimes helps to bring to mind a time or place where we feel such calm restfulness – perhaps while sitting in a park or in our garden or indeed in the armchair.

Just because we have made a resolute determination to stay on the breath, it rarely happens. The day-to-come impinges on us. Our worries, aversions and excitements don't seem to obey our will! Then we may feel tired or restless. Yet we keep noting these states and gently turning away from them back to the breath. And – most important – when we go back to the breath, to repeat that resolution.

This resolution is not hard or harsh as if we are going into battle, but more an encouragement, a cajoling, as we might tempt a child away from some obstinate rebellion. For the monkey mind (the Buddha's description) is, alas, beyond our control such are its unwholesome conditionings. But it does offer us an opportunity to develop gentle patience and calm persistence.

We keep doing this until we feel 'somewhat concentrated' – a favourite phrase of my main Mahasi teacher, Sayadaw U Janaka. In practice, this means it is left entirely up to the meditator. How long it takes depends on our frame of mind. The more restless or sleepy, the longer it may take. But hopefully the preparatory practices of some small ritual and the 'default position' of abiding in calm attentiveness will have helped. But as soon as we know ourselves to be sort of steady, then comes the quality of investigation.

d) Vipassana – developing insight

Having developed 'somewhat' five of the Seven Factors of Awakening, namely calmness especially of the body; steadiness of an alert attention; and equanimity, openness, a passive receptive attitude. Awareness, the controlling factor, is presumed.

Now we raise a question mark in the mind arising out of a desire to know, to understand. This is wonder, the emotion of the philosopher within, a curiosity. This curiosity is looking at something, not looking for something. Its attitude is: 'Am I seeing, feeling, experiencing this as it really is?' It stimulates the joy of interest.

And it raises effort, another factor. Effort is already there, of course, supporting the quality of awareness and steadiness of attention, but checked by calmness. But when curiosity is introduced, one can often feel the energy rising. At this point, should any idea of attaining or achieving something sneak into the process, it will corrupt. We will get tight; feel bored since our desire is not being fulfilled; feel exhausted since the wrong energy does not replenish but keeps drawing on our reserve.

So we need to have the right attitude, second on the Noble Path. That attitude is to have faith in the 'Buddha within', this very intuitive intelligence (paññā) is the active side of awareness (sati). All we have to do is to watch, feel, experience whatever arises and passes away that draws our attention within the field of awareness.

This right attitude includes the intention to investigate the Three Characteristics of Existence. Impermanence, the first, is best seen in the breath. Each in-breath, each out-breath arises only to pass away. Seeing impermanence is to undermine our attachment to what we thought was permanent or continuous. Indeed, it undermines all our attachments since everything is arising and passing away.

Second, we explore the role of a desire based on the understanding that this transient world can deliver true happiness. In meditation, this desire expresses itself by indulging what it finds pleasant, such as when we plan, daydream of love fulfilled and so on. It resists unpleasant experience such as anxiety and guilt. Here lies the psychological reason for our suffering and feelings of unsatisfactoriness.

And third, not-self. This is not a metaphysical proposition such as 'There is no self. 'Instead, it is a teaching tool. As we experience whatever draws our attention it becomes 'an object'. The Intuitive Awareness knows 'it'. There's a feeling of distance from the object. Instead of 'I'm in pain', we note 'pain–there'. There, not here! This separation of the knowing from the known is an initial step towards understanding that what we experience is 'not me, not mine'.

We can prime this curiosity by purposefully seeing one of these characteristics. The Buddha suggests we see the impermanence of the breath. Then we can just watch, just feel, just experience whatever draws our attention. That's enough!

It really is as simple as that. We don't believe it. We always think we have to do something. Try sitting back and watching the show with the curiosity of a child.

For Further clarification, see Guided Meditations
https://www.satipanya.org.uk/audio-video/

e) Metta: developing goodwill – the Theory

First, let's understand the importance of goodwill (metta) practice.

With vipassana-only practice, the inner onlooker, the observer, may become too objective. The true state of vipassana is non-attachment, neither attached nor detached. This is necessary for clear comprehension and close investigation of the Three Characteristics. But if we become too objective, too detached, the equanimity there soon degrades into indifference once we take this position into the world of action.

A woman told me that after practising vipassana her husband found her cold and unresponsive. I suggested she practice metta. The last report was positive.

This is what metta is all about: re-engagement. It is there in the Eightfold Path. After Right Understanding comes right attitude. Whatever wisdom we gain from our practice remains sterile unless translated into an Right Attitude and then, with both this understanding and attitude, we can progress to Right Speech, Right Action and Right Livelihood.

Be careful of confusing this re-engaging with other forms of love. Metta is not attachment. So long as we have a view of self, whatever the love for another some attachment will always be present. It is not erotic love either. And it's not an emotion!

Metta is an attitude. While the heart may respond with warm and delicious feelings, that is a consequence of metta. That's why I prefer the translation of goodwill as opposed to loving-kindness, though it is also that.

Metta is all the virtues we want in a good friend. And sometimes a good friend may tell us something we don't want to hear. Metta allows people to be truthful with us. Likewise we should treat those who dislike us or whom we dislike with the same impartial goodwill. This is the meaning of 'love your enemy'. We don't have to 'love' someone to treat them with metta.

In this way metta is the basic relationship we should have towards everyone. Indeed all beings! It can even affect the way we treat objects. How often have you closed the fridge door gently?

Metta is the default position in our relationship to the world. From this, compassion and joy arise naturally. Would it not be perfectly normal to want to help a friend in distress? And goodwill makes it easy for us to rejoice in a friend's success.

These attitudes – metta, compassion, joy – are called Illimitables. We can develop them indefinitely for there are innumerable beings and the depth of development is unfathomable. Like a number, no matter how big it is, you can always add one.

Underpinning each is equanimity, the other Illimitable, that here means non-attachment or non-prejudice. And all together these four are called the Brahmavihara – Dwelling Place of the Gods. In other words, they are the most bountiful and beautiful heart states we can experience – true of any virtue, in fact.

How often should we practise? All sittings, no matter how long, should end with some metta. At least five minutes. You will find a five-minute metta at the end of both the Detailed Guided Meditation and Metta https://www.satipanya.org.uk/audio-video/

But the Buddha's advice is to practise it all the time, whether standing, walking, sitting or lying down. Whenever there is 'nothing to do' – sitting on a bus, waiting at the traffic lights, climbing stairs – begin the practice. If we were to use up all the 'doing nothing' minutes with metta practice, that alone would change our lives radically for metta is the only true revolutionary force.

Discourse on Metta

> If you are wise and want to reach the state of peace,
> you should behave like this:
> You should be upright, responsible, gentle and humble.
> You should be easily contented and need only a few things.
> You should not always be busy. You should have the right sort of work.
> Your senses should be restrained, and you should be modest.
> You should not be exclusively attached to only a few people.
> You should not do the slightest thing that a wise person could blame you for.
> You should always be thinking: May all beings be happy.
> Whatever living beings there are, be they weak or strong,
> big or small, large or slender, living nearby or far away,
> those who have already been born and those who have yet to be born,
> may all beings without exception be happy.

You should not tell lies to each other.
Do not think that anyone anywhere is of no value.
Do not wish harm to anyone, not even when you are angry.
Just as a mother would protect her only child at the risk of her own life,
so you should let the warmth of your heart go out to all beings.
Let your thoughts of love go through the whole world with no ill-will and no hate.
Whether you are standing, walking, sitting or lying down,
so long as you are awake you should develop this mindfulness.
This, they say, is the noblest way to live.
And if you do not fall into bad ways, but live well and develop insight,
and are no longer attached to all the desires of the senses,
Then truly you will never need to be reborn in this world again.

f) Metta: Developing goodwill– the Practice

We can develop metta in many ways: by chanting the metta discourse in the morning, for example, and the following evening chant taken from a commentary, the Visuddhimagga.

The traditional blessings can be whittled down to four:

> May you be safe (from dangers outside and within us).
> May you be well (free from all sickness and disease).
> May you be happy (free of all mental distress).
> May you enjoy ease of living.
> (May you live contented and in harmony with the world – alternative.)

The sequence of offering starts with :

> our benefactors (with gratitude goodwill arises naturally)
> those who are near and dear
> friends and co-workers
> a neutral person (someone we see, but don't know)
> towards myself
> a difficult person
> those around us
> those in the neighbourhood (think of where you live)
> all in our country
> all in Europe

> all people on earth
> all beings in all directions

g) Developing Forgiveness

Asking for forgiveness: Bring an event or person to mind. Experience the arising states of mind – guilt, shame, remorse, self-justification. Acknowledge how we have caused our own suffering; reflect on the unwholesomeness of these states; apologise; determine not to behave in this way again.

Forgiving: Bring an event or person to mind. Experience the arising states of mind; hurt, revenge, spite. Acknowledge how we have caused our own suffering; reflect on the unwholesomeness of these states; offer forgiveness; determine to forgive in future.

Forgiving oneself: Bring events to mind where we have harmed ourselves: consider the meaning of ignorance and delusion and how they manifest; accept that to suffer the consequences of past actions is enough, no need to punish oneself; determine not to repeat the same folly.

> May All Beings Be Happy!
> Sabbe satta sukhita hontu (x3)
> Sadhu, sadhu, sadhu
> Well done!

Forgiveness exercises accompany the Heartcare (metta) mp3 on website http//www.satipanya.org.uk under Dhamma Talks

h) Resolution

The final part of the morning practice is the act of resolution. Resolution, resolve, determination are all part of the second step of the Eightfold Path – Right Attitude or Right Intention.

If vipassana brings right understanding and metta turns that into Right Attitude, then the act of resolution reinforces both and commits us to a day of determined commitment to Buddhadhamma.

And one day at a time is quite enough. To determine something for a week is possible, but over a month that resolve dissolves unless reinforced. And to determine for a year can be depressing. One day, this day, is feasible. Take care of the minutes and the days will take care of themselves!

It is often the case in our lives that we take on certain commitments and then fail to reinforce their intentions. The situation begins to move away from us and we lose it. A marriage vow given to witnesses lasts that day. From then on presumption leads to laziness and carelessness. Disagreements and annoyances may eventually wither the original vow. Without reinforcing our daily commitment to the work we do, our original enthusiasm slips into apathy. Even more so with the Dhamma for it is constant in its demands and relentless in its labours. It's no easy thing to grow spiritually. The Buddha warns us that this is a 'gradual path'.

What is a resolution then? To understand the role of intention, an intentioned intention, we need to understand Dependent Origination and how we create our own conditioning and kamma. An intention is an idea or thought laced with desire. It may be wholesome or unwholesome, but at the point of intention no karmic act has-been performed. To hold an intention long enough so that we can determine its ethical value is to give us the only real choice we have. I say 'choice' tentatively for who in their right mind would choose to do something that leads to unhappiness.

Once we have agreed to make that choice we have identified with it. This is what 'I' am going to do. There is still no karmic act. Only when that choice becomes action of sustained thought, speech or deed, do we create a kamma. What was it that made manifest a desire, that brought something out of potential into the actual? That force is the will and that is what the Buddha calls kamma (the technical Pali word for action).

Now the original intention has a lot of stored-up energy depending on habitual action or indeed addiction. Anything compulsive – eating, watching TV, social media, talking and talking – is a habit hard to tame because of its accumulated power.

On the other hand, acts of generosity, of service, of truthfulness, of commitment may be weak in energy because they have not been developed through beneficial habit. So a habit in itself is not the problem. What we need to be clear about is its purpose and content.

Of course our personality and character are a collection of these habits – and this determines our destiny. So if we see we are taking the wrong tack, we need to undermine those unskilful, perhaps immoral, habits. And if we see ourselves following a wholesome, virtuous ways then we should reinforce those habits.

That re-enforcement begins with the resolution. And a good time to make a resolution is just at the end of our morning practice where we determine to further our virtue and to undermine unskilful habits.

> 'Today, just this day, I will practise ... live mindfully ... with a good heart ...'

> 'Today, just this day, I will not ... won't go down that road ... refuse to ...'

Repeat these as often as possible throughout the day, but definitely when occasions arise to demand our resolution.

Make them easy to attain so we can congratulate ourselves every evening and slowly we'll go from strength to strength. This is especially true of new year resolutions! And don't be put off by the occasional lapse into old ways. As Ginger Rogers admonished Flatfoot Fred in Swing Time: 'Take a deep breath, pick yourself up, dust yourself off and start all over again!'

4

DEVELOPING THE PERFECTION OF DETERMINATION

Determination, one of the Ten Perfections, is exemplified in the Bodhisatta Siddharttha Gotama's quest to become a Fully Self-Enlightened Buddha, particularly when he sat beneath the Bodhi Tree and determined with resolute resolution to find the answer to his quest or die.

To help strengthen our commitment, we need to contemplate these four areas: Our capability (can); our responsibility (ought); our aspiration (want); and our determination (will) to undermine what is unwholesome and develop what is virtuous.

To begin overcoming an unwholesome conditioning, bring to mind a personal trait you do not consider wholesome, skilful or virtuous.

> a) I am able to, I can resist this temptation: Repeat until there is a conviction of this ability.
>
> b) I ought to resist this for my own benefit and the benefit of others: Repeat until the heart is moved by it.
>
> c) I want to: Repeat until an enthusiasm arises. Where there is resistance, it is spoken kindly to cajole the heart into acceptance. We need to develop ways of encouraging ourselves.
>
> d) And I will resist this temptation whenever it arises: Repeat till one feels the determination in the gut.

In the same way we can determine to develop a virtue: Bring to mind a virtue you want to develop.

    a) I am able to, I can develop this virtue.

    b) I ought to for my own benefit and the benefit of others.

    c) I want to.

    d) I will develop this virtue whenever the occasion arises.

Do this exercise every morning – such practice has an immediate but not a lasting effect. So one has to keep repeating it and the more often the better. We can do this every time an unwholesome or wholesome desire arises. We can go through this process, even if speedily.

Just like the practice of vipassana, metta and constant mindfulness, this practice cannot be stopped until we are fully liberated.

That's the way it is!

5

BREAKFAST AT LAST!

If for some external reason we cannot practise this mindful eating, then make sure we have that quiet cup of tea alone, just us with our body. This can be done whenever we drink or eat, though that first 'break-fast' is a special time for it sets the attitude for the day.

Consider the body's importance, especially since the Buddha pointed to this form of existence as the best to attain liberation. Here we have joys and woes and the intelligence to seek and find the escape. Let us remind ourselves that we cannot be here without a body, that through the body we come to receive knowledge, that we can communicate, relate, take part in society, create good kamma and practise meditation. To feed the body is to nourish a space, sacred specifically to ourselves. The Buddha says this fathom-long body is the world, and it is here we find the causes of suffering and the end to it.

So having made our cup of tea and holding it before us, we seize the chance to reinforce our commitment to the Path of Dhamma. Here at Satipanya we have devised a reflection based on the one the Buddha gave to the Sangha.

> Wisely reflecting, I eat this food not to indulge sensual pleasure or to seek comfort. Being mindful of every mouthful, I shall undermine unwholesome habits and develop appreciative joy.
>
> I eat only to sustain and nourish the body, thinking thus: I will allay hunger without overeating so that I may continue to live blamelessly and at ease.

> This offering brings me health, long life, strength and happiness. May the merits of my practice support the happiness, health, long life, rebirth in the heavenly realms and ultimately the awakening of those who have kindly provided this food.

The final paragraph is a grateful acknowledgement of the efforts of thousands of people and plants – and the sacrifice of animals if you are not a vegetarian – that have brought this food to our table.

Even if we only do the following exercise once a day and that with just a cup of tea, it will keep alive within us the spiritual practice around food. Here's how we do it:

> Closing the eyes, contact the body and get in touch with feelings of thirst or hunger.
>
> Acknowledge that some of those feelings will be natural appetite, the body manifesting its needs, but insidiously intermingled are those feelings of greed.
>
> Making a clear resolution to nourish the body, take the first sip or bite and simply sit back within yourself.
>
> Observe, feel and experience the arising and passing of different tastes, the action of tasting and chewing, all the while mindful of arising delight.
>
> Purposefully intend the action of swallowing, follow the beverage or food and stay with whatever feelings arise. Momentary satisfaction of appetite insidiously intermingled with the gratification of greed!
>
> Wait till 'More!' arises and repeat the process.

At some point the body will emit feelings of 'Enough' and here greed may steal quietly from its hiding place. 'Go on, just this once. Just that one more piece of toast!' Just sitting till that sensual desire passes means we have got the better of the habit of indulgence. Our self-discipline has been strengthened. Our body is healthier for putting its needs first.

When 'More' passes, contentment may arise – the heart without greed. Discerning the difference between contentment and gratification is crucial: One leads to Nibbana, the other to the Realm of Hungry Ghosts! And that realm is right here manifesting as feelings of unsatisfactoriness, of never enough, nagging compulsions and dictatorial addictions.

Buon   appetito!

6

TRAVELLING TO AND FROM WORK

How do we spend our time travelling? Is it an opportunity to practise or a time to get through? In the car, do we turn on the radio, play music?

On public transport, do we do the same or read?

On a long journey, do we do the same?

How much do we daydream?

Whatever we put our attention on, that becomes a means of conditioning. We are creating or reinforcing a habit.

Then the question arises: What sort of habits do we want to develop? I think we would have little objection to wholesome, skilful, virtuous habits. In which case, daydreaming is out. When we daydream, we are carried along by an unwholesome attitude. The thought stream may be beautiful. We may be saving the world from ecological disaster, but it won't bear up to reality. It will be dreaming. So whatever thought we wish to have, we need to make it constructive, deliberate, purposeful thinking. A book helps.

If travelling with a companion, a topic of mutual interest for discussion. Of course, with a companion comes the danger of daydream turning into useless speech. We find it hard to be silent in company. So at least make the conversation beneficial.

Listening to the radio or podcasts presents the same question. What sort of mental state does what I am hearing develop? If we know the input is going to do harm, no matter how little, then we need to find the strength to stop it. It helps if we can replace it with something wholesome.

But the important point is that these times are precious moments for practice. Why waste them? Apart from developing wholesome mental states through reading, listening and conversing, especially when we're on public transport, we can practise metta, vipassana or just abiding peacefully in the present moment.

Continuity of practice produces results. A favourite word of the Buddha was appamādo – diligence! It doesn't take much effort to decide to do something wholesome. Otherwise it is a case of one step forward, two steps back. No wonder we sometimes feel we are getting nowhere.

7

BACK HOME

Back home after a day out, whether at work or for some other reason. It depends on what sort of day it has been, but for sure the worse it was, the less we want to sit.

And what is it we are coming home to?

So many imponderables. Yet to sit quietly for a while, no matter how hard, can truly re-energise the system. For it is a rare day we arrive back suffused and suffusing calm equanimity. And if we were, we would want to sit and deepen the state.

You may be lucky as I was to take public transport. It allows us to sit and rest. Instead of looking mindlessly out of the window, we can sit and let the breath calm or energise us. I have to confess I fell asleep most times and on occasion missed my stop. But I always felt the better for it, even if it meant a long walk home.

If we're returning to a quiet home, take some refreshment, but make time to sit quietly, maybe not in a formal sitting posture. Let the day run through the mind, from the time we left the house till our return. See what we have brought in with us. Is there anxiety there, irritation? Was it an overly busy day, but exhilarating with resultant restlessness? Disappointing and exhausting? Or was it a fulfilling day, satisfying?

If we don't take time for meditation, then there is the near certainty that whatever we have brought home will strengthen dukkha. Unattended disappointment can so easily spiral downward into depression while exhilaration may fool us into grandiose plans and expectations that eventually come crashing down in exhaustion. Very sad.

Whatever state we are in, use the techniques we know to level everything off towards equilibrium. Wait till calm equanimity begins to rise.

If we are returning to a busy house or family home, suggest everyone sit together quietly for a moment. Or if this isn't possible, then perhaps we could ask to be allowed a few minutes' meditation and find a place of quiet to do it.

Always end with metta no matter how short. It is so important to re-engage with the right attitude. Then make resolutions as to how the evening will be skilfully spent.

The Buddha reminds us, 'Life is uncertain. Death is certain.' Let's not waste even a moment.

WORK

1

WORK

What does the word work conjure up for you? Is it a warm glow? Or do you feel a great weight descend? Are you filled with bright energy or the burning energy of stress, frustration and anxiety?

The Buddha gave Right Livelihood such importance that he has placed it right there in the Eightfold Path. He could have included it in Right Action, but no, he gives it its own importance.

More broadly, we need to ask ourselves what we are doing with our life. Do we feel we are wasting it? Or do we feel we are wasting our life at work? For most of us that's around 40 hours a week – and our most energetic time.

There is within us a spiritual calling, something demanding to be, to be developed. These days we think of spiritual calling as something to do with becoming a religious, a nun or monk. But in the Christian Middle Ages, it was understood that God had called you to a profession or skill, usually what your family was already involved in. It is the modern separation of the secular from the spiritual that has caused so much of our malaise. Once the accent is put on the secular then we are into the 'things of this world' – riches, fame, power and pleasure. A life devoted to these must necessarily end in disappointment if only because it will all pass away. When we put the spiritual back into the secular, the whole world of work takes on a completely different nature. It becomes a spiritual workshop.

How does the spiritual manifest in Right Livelihood? In some people it is so strong, it is felt to be a calling, a vocation. I knew a child of five who told me she was going to be a doctor and that's what she became. For others, it's not so strong, but a general feeling of doing what they were meant to be doing with their lives. Then there are those who live in confusion as to what they should be doing and wait hopefully for inspiration or to be told that something will turn up. And others have no hope of making sense of their work life. It is a means to earn money so they can do what they want to do after work.

A great deal of our work life depends on society and the economic situation. We may very well have experienced all four types just mentioned. At one or other time inspired, feeling content, depressed and lost about our work situation. Indeed we may suffer these very same swings in the very job we are doing – even in one day!

So the first thing we have to do, if we have not already done so, is to make a determination to turn our present work, no matter whether we enjoy it or not or whether we think it is meaningful or not, into a spiritual practice.

Not sure how to go about doing that?

If we see our working lives as a service towards the employer, the other employees, clients, society as a whole and, of course, to ourselves, then our work takes on a meaning transcendent of itself. It doesn't matter what we do, from the menial to the extraordinary, all are there for a greater purpose than the actual work itself. It connects us and paradoxically makes is us feel whole.

2

SUCCESS AND FAILURE : TRIAL AND ERROR

I am not sure I should be confessing this, but my life is a catalogue of failures. Failure, of course, is what happens when we don't succeed. It's a pretty depressing state. As the realisation of failure dawns or hits us between the eyes, there's that shock moment when the stomach sinks. And then the nausea followed by anger and hatred towards those succeeded where we failed or the system that beat us. We experience soul searching, self-recrimination, along with the further woundings of guilt and shame and into the yawning chasm of despair. Indeed, failure is always a painful experience. We shouldn't be surprised at this. After all it's a mini-death that can at worst lead to suicide, such as the French chef who shot himself when newspaper reports suggested his restaurant might lose its three Michelin stars.

Defining failure always leads us to a measurement against success, to a comparison with how it ought to have been. But what task did we set ourselves? A sanguine character will tend to overreach. Even the most circumspect and morose often expect what is beyond their capabilities or more than the situation can deliver.

In Christian spiritual language, however, this failure is known as a humiliation but not in the belittling sense, rather a sharp correction to 'the way it really is'. In times past, to be humble meant to know oneself. It did not mean to be weak and worthy of beating. Humility is another word for 'know thyself'.

Aiming at success always carries the danger of overreach because it is the self trying as always to accumulate. And the more it has, the safer it feels whether it be riches, power, fame or simply pleasures. It invests itself in the project and defines itself by its success. You'll always find these three factors: Over-aiming, emotional attachment and identity. When we fail, we suffer to some extent an identity crisis, emotional turmoil and loss. In despair we may give up, become despondent. And life stagnates. Is there another way we can approach our goals for we do not want to lose our aspirations, be it relationships, work, spiritual aims?

Suppose we change the language. Suppose we look at life as a challenge and an exploration, rather than success, competition and possible failure. Suppose we talk of trial and error. Surely now the world changes. We are no longer in a world of conflict. We are working on a hypothesis like any scientist. We are co-operating with the world to see if our idea will work or not. It may work out, it may not. No matter.

Writer Samuel Beckett got it right when he said: 'Try again. Fail again. Fail better.' (I'm presuming Beckett is here using the word 'fail' as in trial and 'error'.) Writing is an exacting art. Indeed so is all creative pursuit. One never quite expresses what one wants. True art is all trial and forever error, for the real never meets with the ideal but that doesn't mean a piece of work may not give satisfaction. Yet try again we must. The Buddha tried over and over and in so many ways to express the Dhamma. People were forever misinterpreting his words. Yet we say all the teachings are just pointing the way. The finger points to the moon. There's nothing to be gained by looking at the end of the finger!

Seeing life as trial and error excludes us from the pains of failure. Once the error has played itself out, a fallow period follows, a time for regeneration, not barrenness, where the former desire to explore possibilities resurfaces. Creativity is natural to all nature. Nature does not deal in success and failure. It's about finding growth in any given situation. We are rooted in a world that is forever creating. How foolish not to join the party!

3

CREATING SPACE – ENERGY

We live in a society that puts a price on time. It was not always so. But that's how it is at present and for us it's not simply a case of living with it, but of living wisely with it. The growing demands of efficiency and productivity strain the last ounce of energy each moment has. And that force is, in fact, our life-energy. Our work can demand the better part of our inner resources at the expense of personal welfare, family and social life. If this resonates to any extent, then we'll need to learn how to conserve energy. Try creating space, temporal space.

Renowned meditation master Ajahn Thate succinctly expresses the spiritual life: 'Take it easy. Make it simple. Stay with the one who knows.'

a) Do one job at a time.

Actually, we can't do two jobs at the same time but that's what we try to do. Who hasn't found themselves having a conversation with someone and filling in a form and/or writing up a piece of work and/or working on the computer? Occasionally, we get away with it when engaged in an automatic manual task, but it's still taxing the brain. Even if we are expert multi-taskers, it's still necessary to fully attend to the task at hand. Failing to do so gives rise to mistakes and causes accidents.

So it's one task at a time for us. That means paying attention to what we are doing. The effect is to increase our focus and span of attention. That is, our concentration is enhanced.

b) Create a pause between every task.

The phone rings. Do we immediately launch ourselves at it? Do we notice how mobile calls trump everything else? This compulsive behaviour simply increases our agitation. And agitation is wasted energy.

At the end of a task, STOP, reflect on what has been done. Acknowledge it. Put it aside. Take a breath and relax. Let this be as long as it takes to feel inwardly calm. Most often it's less than a minute. And then we intend the next task and remind ourselves of our Dhamma intention (see below).

Take the phone call, for instance. Surely most people will wait for three to five rings. At the first ring, we just acknowledge where we are with our work. At the second, we stop and breathe, at the third calmly pick up the phone. Should the caller ring off, call the person back.

If we can begin each task with a mind uncluttered, with clarity, our efficiency is increased.

That should make the powers that be happy!

    c)   Take a silent break.

Tea breaks and lunch breaks are times to really establish that quiet equanimity and still mindfulness that the morning meditation put us in touch with. Again, it doesn't have to be long. Five minutes may be enough before we join others.

It's also so refreshing to get away from the workplace for a while, sit in the local park or just quietly walk the streets or as I used to do, sit in the local church.

    d)   Go with the flow.

I once received a card with a fish floating in a river and the caption 'only dead fish go with the flow'. But in reality we're as if dead if we lose our sense of present mindfulness. Should the river be in torrent or flood, then we will surely be lost if we don't exercise still awareness.

Going with the flow means being able to let go of what we're doing when something needs to be attended to. That phone call again, that colleague approaching, at home the child calling for attention - these can all seem unwelcome irritating interruptions. Any form of anger is wasted energy.

    e)   A Dhamma intention.

This could be anything. For instance, before we answer the phone we might remind ourselves to speak kindly, openly and appropriately.

There we have it. Five simple tips that help us work better, feel better and conserve our life energy.

Easy, weasy, peasy!

4

CREATING SPACE – EMOTIONS

Along with temporal space we have emotional space, the ability to drop back into a spacious heart, the state of equanimity. The greater the emotional upsurge, the more important this is.

    a) When we are in a rush, stop and let it all subside.

The alarm fails and we find ourselves speed washing, gobbling breakfast, running to the bus stop or driving with hands clenched to the steering wheel. Even if we arrive in time for work, that anxiety rush stalks us through the day. It's as if we've put ourselves on a rollercoaster and don't know how to get off.

A shot of vipassana can be most useful here. Find those few minutes to sit down, close the eyes and let everything calm down. Say to those around: 'I just need a few minutes to collect myself. To chill out!'

When I was working as a teacher this had a great effect on me. I often found myself in rushing mode, trying to get things done. I got in the habit of stopping, if only for a moment, and found it useful to talk myself down.

Down to what? Equanimity which is stillness of the body, calmness of the heart, silence of the mind and an attitude of openness. From here we can bring in metta or goodwill intention and start again calmly.

    b) Working with a persistent mental state.

By stopping the rush and stilling ourselves, we can encounter a deeper mental state such as anxiety, boredom, depression and restless energy. These emotional states may hang around all day. For some people, they are virtually a constant.

When we don't have the time to do vipassana, we can set them aside. This is not the same as suppression, because that presumes negativity towards these feelings, ignoring them because we don't want to feel them. But by setting them aside, we acknowledge them with the intention of managing them at a more appropriate time. In this way we don't add aversion to the mix. Indeed, we can do this with kind gentleness as if bandaging a sore knee and yet we keep walking.

Of course, it is then important to find a time in the day when we can work with them. And this is better done as soon as you get home from work before eating, even if only for 20 minutes.

Something to pin on the wall, place on the desk. Adjust according to personal experience.

One Job at a Time

Intend New Action

Make Dhamma Resolve

Steady Attention, Season with Care

Bring back Wandering Mind with Gentle Insistence

STOP

Let Reactions Subside

One Job Well Done!

5

CREATING SPACE – ATTENTION

After a disturbing event or encounter, wait for the reaction to subside.

When we sit in vipassana, we are instructed to watch, feel and experience anything that draws our attention. We're meant to be focused yet loose, not attached or caught up in any particular object. So if we are experiencing pleasant states, a sudden pain in the knees is simply something else to turn our attention to. If our calm concentration is such that we are locked onto the breath and someone sneezes, we're not supposed to desire the annihilation of that person's nose, but to observe, 'hearing, hearing' and to note any reaction that might arise.

Why can't we be like this at home and at work? We happen to be getting on with job, feel pressured even, and someone comes. They may come calmly and excuse themselves, but often they are loud, in a rush or an irritated state. Are we irritated? Do we feel panicked? Do we despair?

Let's bring the lesson of vipassana directly into our lives. Even when we are working under considerable pressure or with enthusiasm and no wish to be disturbed, we can still be relaxed. We just have to remind ourselves that someone may arrive, asking for our attention.

When that happens, we ask for a moment, acknowledge where we are and, most important, the person's mood. It may demand patience. Then turn the attention entirely to the person. No fuss. No wasted energy.

This practice helps us to be completely open to what they are offering. Should it be anger, anxiety or another unpleasant state, we need to feel it and listen to them. Their emotional state can resonate strongly within us and we need to hold steady instead of reacting with equal impatience or anxiety. I have found it most helpful to listen to what they are saying more than attend to what they are feeling. That way I find it easier to remain equanimous and then to genuinely answer their concern.

If, of course, they arrive quietly and calmly, then note how that brings out the best in us. So, if we find ourselves irritated and rushing, we remind ourselves that this is not the way to get the best out of someone. Let's attend to our own state and wait till it calms.

If we fail to behave skilfully or we lose it somewhere in the middle, then we need to give that mental state the time it needs to subside. If we constantly revisit the event in thought and imagination, it tends to escalate. When this happens, keep stopping, contact the feeling and give it time to burn out, even if only a little.

Bringing the practice into our daily life in this way, increases our sense of calm and equanimity.

6

LIMITS OF POWER AND MISSION CREEP

Nothing makes the self feel more comfortable than more – of anything. This is especially so of power: 'I am in control.'

Every job has its boundary and description. At the interview we want to know what is expected of us. First, we are satisfied with just doing the job which may be taxing initially but after a while we feel on top of the work – we're in control. We enter a period of ease.

Then gradually possibilities begin to creep in. And with all the goodwill in our hearts we do something outside our job description. And we are astonished how it causes such hurt and anger.

Jack starts to work for a charity in accounts. Before long he realises the website could be better. He knows a website designer whom he thinks is very good and invites them to meet the boss – without any prior consultation. The next morning the boss is visibly angry when Jack tells him what he has done. Out of goodwill the boss sees the designer and nothing comes of it. Jack feels snubbed. A distance grows between them. Again without anything being said, things return to where they were. But has Jack understood that his goodwill was seen as mission creep? That his actions encroached on another's work? That he did not consider his boss's position?

I must confess I was very good at this and my manager accused me of wanting her job! I didn't. Honestly! It cost me an apology and a box of chocolates. As it happened, when she moved up I was offered her job – by which time, of course, I did want it. So I must have got something right.

Similarly, if we are in charge, expanding our remit can undermine others. At some point before we start work we might remind ourselves of our job description and its boundaries. Since I set up Satipanya, this practice has become all too important for me because I have a tendency to do everything myself. This undermines those we have asked to help and generally puts them off offering us assistance in the future.

So what we have here is a basic manifestation of the self as power. It wants to be in control and gives itself any good reason to do so. It never really takes into account the other, save in that the other serves its purpose. No matter how goodwilled the self is, it always turns the other into an object in order to achieve its desire.

To understand the reaction of others to our goodwill mission creep, check out how it feels when someone does that to us.

And really, what harm is there in consultation?

SOME WHOLESOME AND SOME UNWHOLESOME QUALITIES

1
THE TOUGH NUT

I'm sure you know what your own 'tough nut' is. I know a little about them since I took a couple of cars apart in those halcyon days when I had nothing better to do. You have to apply WD40 and, sometimes, welly.

There's usually a habit – unwholesome, of course – we retreat to when things go bad or even a bit off. It could be around eating or sex or drugs or sleep or alcohol or any number of more or less unwholesome pursuits.

But we begin to realise that it doesn't deal with the original problem. So it becomes an obsession and addiction, and then a problem in itself. It can become an escape route so entrenched that it will probably be the last to be filled out and transformed.

There are many self-help books, therapies and systems such as the 12-step programme used for alcohol and drug addiction. But here I'm addressing a more normal level of addiction. Even though I say normal it can be equally tenacious. Even giving up that extra piece of toast can bring tears to the eyes.

As meditators we know the key lies in tanha, wrong desire and craving. It's catching the moment that it arises, before it is energised by action – this is the key to overcoming it. Once we've even started to shift a foot towards the biscuit tin, it's difficult to pull back: 'Just one!' We're easily fooled.

This is why that bright mindfulness is so necessary. It catches the arising of a desire. Right mindfulness is accompanied by calmness. So there's no rush. There's time. We can inwardly stop, watch and feel the energy rise and wait patiently till it subsides.

When we know the conditions for such desires to arise; when we know when, where and/or with whom; that's when we prick the inner ear, gather the inner resolution and stand firm.

We need a ploy to remove ourselves from the scene of possible folly, a wholesome distraction. Listen to music, read a book, watch good TV, call a friend. The danger of suppression is there, of course, if we don't find time to investigate it in meditation. Perhaps the best tactic is to take the 'dog' for a walk. It gets us away from the object of desire and allows us to 'vipassana' the mental state.

And should we find ourselves dashing along the addictive escape route, let's at least not be routed! What then is required? Persistence. Dogged perseverance.

2

IMPULSIVE OR SPONTANEOUS?

When we act impulsively, we do so out of habit. It is a thoughtless reaction: There's no reflection involved. The word impulsive suggests lack of skilfulness. We often regret what we have done.

Somebody asks us to help in the garden and we find ourselves saying: 'Yes, I'd love to!' Immediately that sinking feeling surfaces, we really don't want to do it, we don't have the time. We would prefer to do something else. It scratches at the mind. We think of excuses.

It can lead to fibbing: 'Woke up feeling terrible. I've got a job to do. Someone I must see. Forgot all about it.'

We are prolific in our apologies, but left with an uncomfortable feeling: The dread of being found out, the shame of it.

There's a Mullah Nasruddin story. He is tired of his neighbour asking to use his donkey. So on the next request, he tells him someone else is using the animal. Just then the donkey brays. And when his neighbour raises an eyebrow, he asks: 'Who are you going to believe? Me or my donkey?'

We all want to be spontaneous. It suggests skilfulness and joy. We think spontaneity should arise spontaneously! But it's hard work to train ourselves towards a genuine, unaffected naturalness about what we do. Consider sport. How many times do tennis players practise their shots? And in the immediacy of the game their strokes are spontaneous, though maybe not always as accurate as they would wish. Consider performance artists whether actors or musicians. Although their performance seems natural, enormous practice has been engaged in beforehand.

So it is with virtues. We need to consciously develop them – goodwill, generosity, patience and so on. And then every so often we shall surprise ourselves at our spontaneous, wise and joyful response.

3

JOY!

In spring, the daffodils bring a sense of joy. Joy is an Illimitable along with love, compassion and equanimity and just like them it can be developed without boundary, limitlessly.

Often in a rushed and overly busy day or a slow, dull one, our attention fixates on the downers. But notice the times when a form of happiness arises. Often if we are used to excitement we miss out on the sweetness of a quiet joy. Excitement is its subtle enemy for it is an expression of that desire to be happy in an overly emotional way. In other words, high!

Quiet, peaceful joy often arises, but because we are so used to joy as excitement, we miss it and fail to appreciate it. Perhaps it comes when, after some engagement, there is that quiet cup of tea; or while walking from here to there in a park or along a quiet street; or stopping and resting from what we are doing for a moment. When we notice this calm joy, we say to ourselves: 'I am feeling a calm joy.' Sit with it, appreciate its qualities, notice how we feel gently energised by it, not just physically but mentally.

Then when we are settled in it and have drunk our fill, we offer the cup to others and to all beings: 'May you be joyful and may your joy increase!' After all, a joy shared is a joy squared for now we are happy because others are happy.

Then there's the power of positive thinking – a practice the Buddha was very keen on. Even when you feel down, you can note that and then offer yourself a blessing: 'May my unhappiness decrease. May my unhappiness come to an end.' After a while, offer the same blessings to all beings. And then set it aside. Offer joyful blessings to yourself, something sympathetic to oneself. As you begin to lift, offer it to all beings.

This is a much better strategy than one offered by self-pity and resignation: 'I am depressed. I am so depressed. May all beings be depressed.' Or at work: 'I'm bored. I'm so bored. May all beings die of boredom.'

Throughout the day, train yourself in lifting the heart with goodwill intentions of joy and see how you feel at the end of the day.

4

THANK YOU

What a heart-warming, heart-delighting virtue is gratitude! But how often do we contemplate the blessings of what we have received? How often do we consider the many unasked-for graces and fortunes that have come our way? How often has a thank-you been heartfelt and not just a social nicety?

Anyone who has entered the Dhamma and reflected on the supreme gift of this life form, the most advantageous for liberation, cannot help feeling an aching gratitude towards our parents. Many of us may harbour grudges about our upbringing. But do we imagine our parents to be awakened beings? One person said to me that only when he became a parent did he stop complaining about his parents. The Buddha said that even if we carried our parents on our shoulders all our lives, we would not have repaid the gift of life they gave us. Thank you!

What about the gifts we receive from our society? Our whole early education is paid for by others. Both the education system and the National Health System emerged from a desire to educate and heal, from the ideals of egalitarianism and compassion.

What about the police? Do we ever feel gratitude when we see a policeman or a police car? No matter what our opinion of the police might be, we still need them to keep law and order.

And our politicians? Do we really expect them to be saints? Most enter with idealism. They really do want to do something for society – no matter how misguided we may think they are. Would we do any better?

It's not that gratitude should blind us to faults. For instance, gratitude cannot, of course, be given to politicians whose ethics run contrary to the Dhamma. Yet exercised skillfully it balances our more 'natural' tendency to criticise, moan and complain. So what about a bit of appreciation? Or praise?

So thank you!

What about the gifts of friends, workmates, countryside and parks, museums and libraries, public toilets and a myriad other things. Thank you!

And our practice even allows us to see those who dislike us and do us harm as our teachers. Thank you!

Even when things go wrong: We lose our spouses, partners, friends, our jobs. We can see this as 'an opportunity for growth' – even if we say it through bared teeth. Thank you!

And there are things that represent the imagination, skills and work of hundreds of people. Next time we are holding the mobile phone, just think how many people were involved in getting the basic materials, in the design and manufacture, in distribution. We can do it with food, clothes, the humble doorstop. An eternity of thank yous!

And what about the body that carries us around all day? The mind that can be so clear and precise? The heart that can fill our interior with such delight? Let's not dwell on the empty half of the bottle. Thank you!

Gratitude engenders a generous heart. And when our gifts do not carry the heavy labels of 'me' and 'mine', then truly we are renouncing what time and wealth we could have spent on ourselves. So we also develop the virtue of renunciation.

In this simple way the virtuous circle of gratitude, generosity and renunciation twirl us gently towards liberation. This is a path in itself.

Meister Eckhart, the 13th century mystic, maintained that to say thank you all the time would be enough.

If gratitude is not something that comes easy to us, try spending a day saying thank you to everyone and everything and see how we feel by the end of it.

5
NEED SUFFICIENCY GREED

In a time of rampant consumerism and designer label consciousness, it's harder for us to isolate the essentials needed to lead a good and healthy life. So the austerity years recently laid upon us have had one positive in that they offered us the opportunity to gain insight into what is truly necessary and what is not.

What do we really need? The Buddha defined Four Requisites without which the monastic life would be impossible.

> Monastics should be happy with the food offered to them.

But from a lay point of view, what does the body need. Tiramisu? Not that I'm arguing against tiramisu, you understand. Heaven forbid! But when we look at our eating habits, what do we genuinely need for nourishment and a healthy body? Not as much as we think, surprisingly. And what is more, good fresh food is untaxed and therefore, comparatively cheaper than other consumer goods. But it does mean we have to cook for ourselves.

> As for shelter, the foot of a tree.

Well, that's okay in the tropics, but what do we need other than roof over our heads and basic heating? Are fine furnishings vital? Do we walk around our house in mid-winter in a tea shirt?

Then there's clothing.

> Monks are to be content with clothing sewn together from rags.

Just open up to the fullness of your wardrobe and shoe rack. Make sure you have a glass of water handy.

Finally, medicine.

The Buddha asked his monastics to be content with fermented cow's urine.

I'd have to be pretty desperate to go for that one. But consider what a wonderful communal gift the NHS is, especially today when a sense of compatriotism, of citizen communion is so lacking. Do we take it for granted? Do we find nothing but fault?

Suppose we were suddenly given five minutes to evacuate because of a tsunami. What would we take with us? Presuming one has considered this before, I dare say we would take only what we really do need.

Then there is the idea of sufficiency. This is a little more lenient. It's the old adage of 'moderation in all things'. We need clothes for work, clothes for leisure and clothes for pottering about. Food is often a case of conviviality and celebration. Shelter is also home. And we should try to get medicine best to cure our ill health.

This is not an exhaustive list of consumer goods. One obvious exception is transport. And this reminds us that sufficiency isn't only about a personal struggle with greed, but also about our relationship to the earth and so to other people.

If we approach sufficiency from need, we probably have a better measure of moderation.

Otherwise there is greed or if you prefer – retail therapy!

6

DIGNITY

Just for a moment before you read this, sit in a way that you feel dignified, that expresses the word dignity.

Can you describe to yourself the physical qualities? How does the heart feel? What happens at the thought level?

We associate the word with royalty and there is a danger we might confuse it with superiority. That's when the little devil of comparison sneaks in: 'All comparison is odious'!

Is there a feeling of self-worth, a worthiness free of status, wealth, fame, beauty?

There was time we had dustbin men. As a boy I watched them lift the heavy metal bins, slinging them onto their shoulders and heaving the rubbish into an open truck. Their leather backs were mired with slops and filth. They seemed embarrassed. They didn't like me looking at them, didn't want to be noticed. They preferred the dark winter mornings. I didn't sense even then that they were happy with their task. They were at the bottom of the working class. My dad used to leave them a fiver for Christmas.

These days bin collection is clean, motorised and most refuse collectors wear official clothing. They are part of the growing importance of recycling. Most own their own homes. The ones that service us are happy to have a chat. They think of themselves as middle class.

But when our dignity arises dependent on social conditions, it is fragile. Should those conditions change, our dignity feels damaged. But when our dignity comes from within, only we can damage it.

True dignity sits beyond our social status. The most menial worker can have the dignity of a king.

When King Bimbissara of Maghada first saw the Buddha on alms round, he was greatly impressed by his bearing. That was the beginning of a lifelong friendship as disciple and supporter.

This inner sense of dignity is based on goodness and brings with it a sense of self-worth.

Sitting in a dignified manner, is the body upright? Floppy? Tense or relaxed?

Repeating the word dignity to oneself, check whether the heart is troubled, restless, dull? Or gentle, calm, serene? Is the mind agitated or silent?

Walk about a bit. Get the feel of 'dignity' – not superiority!

Can you take it to work?

7

PITY SORROW COMPASSION

Pity – feeling sorry for: I'm using this term in its negative sense. When we hear ourselves say, I pity Jack, how does this 'I' define itself? There may be a genuine sorrow for the person and their situation, but somehow this 'I' stands apart from it. It is saying to itself: 'He does deserve it, he's such an idiot. I'd never get myself into that situation. Thank heaven I'm not like that.' A smug satisfaction is lurking along with, but quietly ignored, a sense of schadenfreude, joy in another's suffering.

Being unaware of these subliminal feelings, doesn't mean they have no effect. I'm sure we've heard that false tone in another's voice, that affectation of sorrow on the face. But are we aware when we also pity someone?

It's often a case that in vipassana, if we honestly note what the mind is thinking, that we wake up to these hitherto quietly suppressed attitudes that don't fit into our esteemed self-definition.

Sorrow is a genuine feel for the suffering of another. It can actually be felt as a direct resonance of the other's pain, both psychological and physical. I know someone who felt her daughter's pain when she broke her arm. She had to have her arm in a sling. The daughter felt nothing. This form of sorrow is rare, of course, but we're all touched when we see someone suffer, especially a child or animal for their innocence and vulnerability add poignancy to the situation.

In Calcutta once I turned a corner to see a little girl squatting in the dry dirt road sucking on a black-brown desiccated banana skin. To this day I can still feel the shock in my heart. But did it move me to act?

For me, that's the difference between sorrow and compassion. Compassion is the desire to alleviate suffering. It moves one to action. Anything – even if it is only to influence another to do something.

I'm sorry to say I did nothing to help that little girl and am left with an unrequited sorrow – the penalty when sorrow does not transform into compassion.

So, since the delusion of self is always active, how might we proceed? We acknowledge the conceit of pity, but don't denigrate ourselves for it. It's enough to acknowledge it and determine not to act on it. To feel instead the genuine sorrow and to act on that. In this simple way, our pity diminishes and our compassion grows.

8

SUBLIMATION

Sublimate comes from the Latin sublimare, to lift up. Science uses it to describe the action of a solid evading the liquid state to become a gas. Ice, for instance, turns into water before it vaporises, whereas naphthalene, the smelly bit in mothballs, does so without becoming a liquid.

In right attitude, the second step of the Eightfold Path, the Buddha lists three sublimations: from selfishness to generosity, from aversion to love and from cruelty to compassion. There's no in-between state. The word transformation could be used too but sublimation signals rising higher – towards the sublime.

The Four Illimitables, with no perceived extent to which they can be developed, are love, compassion, joy and peace. They are also called Brahmavihara, The Dwelling Place of the Highest Gods, that is the most sublime of exalted states of mind.

The important insight is to see that it happens naturally. In Zen they say that with wisdom compassion arises naturally. As we purify the mind of its delusion and the heart of its negativity, all that is negative sublimates into its opposite.

Vipassana has a key role here for when we are in contact with the raw feelings of an unwholesome emotion or mood, we are allowing it to sublimate. The real insight is the realisation that we don't have to do anything! It happens all on its own – yet another insight into not-self, not me. What we have to do, of course, is to bear patiently with it, feel it, observe it. We have to attend to it. For sublimation can only happen within awareness, otherwise negativity remains suppressed. Therefore, we need to open up to our inner demons.

This doesn't mean we should not actively develop virtue. The Buddha tells us in the Metta Sutta, the Discourse on Goodwill, that we do need to develop all the attitudes associated with love. He uses a mother's love for her children to illustrate this:

> Just as a mother protects with her child at the risk of her own life,
> So one should cherish all living beings.

We can understand metta here to be love in its widest sense, love as in how we develop our connection with all beings and the world as right relationship. And the sublimation of negative, unwholesome states is a necessary part of this process.

9

RIGHTEOUS ANGER : PLAIN ANGER

Righteous anger does not exist in the Buddha's teaching. All anger is unwholesome and unskilful. We may get what we want, but a price must be paid.

We talk about assertiveness and aggression. This is such a useful distinction to make as assertiveness arises out of equanimity, compassion – and righteousness.

We have forgotten the old maxim to count to 10 before we act in anger. For anger will always distort, mainly by exaggeration. Allowing the anger to abate means a balanced view returns. We can see the situation from the other's point of view. This means we are equanimous or impartial.

To see the other's point of view is an act of love, of compassion and it allows the other to be heard. When someone is heard, their anger usually subsides.

And there is a right view about things. We should stand by our understandings, but not in a tight way. It may be the other has something to say which modifies our view, if only a little.

If we maintain our mindfulness when we are angry, we will feel the heat arise in the chest. We'll feel a tightness – the first signs of attack. We'll see the beginnings of angry intentions. At that point, relax the body. Breathe in deeply and breathe out slowly. No need to make it obvious. If the situation is too much, it's often best to excuse oneself.

But what if someone is angry with us? Before you react with anger, take your attention to what they are saying, not how they are saying it. Give them all the time they need. When they have finished, we indicate that we've been listening. Then we answer appropriately and calmly: 'You've got the wrong person.' 'Are you sure ...?' 'Sorry, I didn't realise ...'

My first job was as a rep for a company making audio-visuals for school. At one school a teacher came blazing at me, accusing us of illegal practices. I remember I quickly apologised if this were true. I asked to phone the boss who said there had been a misunderstanding or mistake and all money would be repaid. The teacher went out of his way to introduce me to other members of staff.

What if you work in an office and abuse spews down the phone? Same as above, but I hear so much about this, that maybe it's time for zero tolerance. Try this: let the person express their anger. Then remain silent. They should come back with something along the lines: 'Are you listening?' or 'Are you there?' Then say calmly: 'I understand what you're saying. And I can understand why you are angry. But can I ask you to phone back when you are in a calmer mood so that we can talk about this rationally?' Or perhaps we signal in a way that is comfortable for us that we're not prepared to bear the anger and put the phone down.

10

DISCIPLINE : SELF-DISCIPLINE

Discipline is one of those Victorian words we don't like the sound of, with its sense of corporal punishment. But that's not where the word began.

It's always interesting to return to the root word and see how it alters with usage and time. The Latin disciplina means instruction and knowledge. The one who wanted it was called a discipulus/a disciple. By the Middle Ages it meant 'mortification by scourging oneself'! A harsh way of developing self-discipline. Today it means 'the practice of training people to obey rules and orders and punishing them if they do not' OED.

In none of the Buddha's teachings is there punishment. He found self-mortification to be just more suffering. Yet he demands the highest level of self-discipline of his ordained Sangha. And of the lay Sangha a set of training rules which when followed diligently, establish a platform for purification.

So how can we develop self-discipline without beating ourselves up? Or getting someone else to beat us up?

First, find a definition for discipline that encapsulates our aim. Our spiritual objective is twofold: To abandon unwholesome habits and develop beautiful ones; and to develop the inner strength to do this.

Here, the training of dolphins may help. When the animal fails to do a trick such as jumping through a hoop, trainers do not criticise, but ignore the mistake and renew their encouragement. On completion of the trick a present is given – a form of positive reinforcement that works just as well on humans.[1]

There's little gain in blaming oneself, in unkind self-criticism, self-recrimination, threatening oneself. When we act unwholesomely, it's good to rest with the inner consequences. A sense of failure, shame, guilt, remorse, anger and so on may arise. Bearing with this is the 'punishment'. No need to pile on further misery. What is more, the action was done. We determine to bear the consequences equanimously. That's sufficient. And to put right what was wrong where possible is all that's asked of us. Then we make a firm resolution not to do that again.

Finally, consider how we might treat ourselves when we overcome a temptation. No matter how many times we fall back into the old habit, we keep repeating this process until slowly but surely, old unskilful habits lose their power.

In a touching discourse, the Buddha teaches Rahula – his young son aged seven who took the lower ordination, samanera – about the dangers of lying. He is gentle and progressive, always appealing to the boy's better nature. The Buddha does not call him

bad or denounce his actions as those of a devil. This is how we should talk to the child within us. In time, Rahula became fully liberated.[2]

When we do something wholesome, in the same way we accept the inner consequences of joy and delight. This is our just reward, our treat. We must of course be careful not to do something wholesome to feel good. But putting aside this error, we accept that our inner atmosphere, the heart's delight, is our treat from wholesome actions. That's enough. Whatever the praise or gift, let it be a welcome consequence of reciprocal joy and gratitude, but never our purpose.

Again the Buddha delights in another's success. Witness his exclamation when Kondañña achieves insight into Nibbana after the first discourse, The Turning of the Wheel of the Law.

---

[1] Dolphin http://understanddolphins.tripod.com/dolphintraining.html

[2] See Ambalatthika-Rahulovada Suttanta (The Ambalatthika Exhortation to Rahula) in this BPS Wheel Publication No.33: http://www.bps.lk

'Then the Blessed One exclaimed: "Truly Koṇḍañña knows. He really knows." And that is how Ven Koṇḍañña acquired the name Añña-Koṇḍañña – Koṇḍañña, the One-Who-Knows.'

Similarly, we can assume the Buddha's character within us and gently coax ourselves towards a consummate, gentle self-discipline, rejoicing in our development of virtue.

11

UNFORGIVINGNESS

Unforgivingness is yet another form of hatred. We have been injured in some way. We feel hurt. We are angry with and hate what the person did and we are angry with and hate the person who did it.

We might be happy to forgive, if only they would say sorry and we believe they mean it. We might be happy for them just to voice it.

Sometimes this won't do because we want an act of genuine contrition. We want reparation – an offering in kind, a small gift. Anything so long as there is a gesture.

Sometimes this won't do either. Our anger and hatred demand compensation equal to the wrongdoing, but more. We say we don't want revenge. We just want them to know the suffering they caused us. This might teach them a lesson. We often call this justice.

Sometimes the suffering as punishment we impose – perhaps withdrawal of support, favour, friendship, in some cases of freedom or even life – may gratify us. But more often it does not because acting out of anger and hatred simply feeds that attitude. We don't feel they have suffered enough.

'Justice has been done.' But justice is a malleable notion. There is no universally accepted punishment for a crime. For similar crimes, some societies hang or maim people, others call this barbaric. The leniency of some societies is seen by others as weak and ineffectual.

The people we know who have injured us, no matter how slightly, may not be the only ones we need to forgive. What about the big players also – the politicians, corporations, bankers, 'them'?

And those who say 'I can't forgive' are expressing a child's 'can't'. They really mean, I won't.

Actual pain or damage to the body whether slight or severe is one thing, but negative, unwholesome reaction to it is our own self-made suffering. Even so we can justly claim compensation for harm done.

Although a sorrow comes from pain or loss via any form of violence to oneself or to the other (broken limbs, acid in the face, a murdered relative), grief is a measure of attachment. Sorrow is the sadness at the needless pain or loss of life that should move us towards compassion, even for the perpetrator and further afield to undermine the causes of violence. Knowing the difference is crucial to bring closure. All grief, anger and revenge are reactions by the aggrieved.

Forgiving, then, begins by refusing to act out of anger and hatred. It is made easy once we realise that the hurt and grief we feel are self-generated and need time and vipassana (insight) to dissolve. We injure our own hearts and when we realise this even an apology from the other is not necessary for forgiveness.[3]

Here's the Buddha:

> 'He abused me, he hit me, he overpowered me, he robbed me.'
> Those who indulge such thoughts do not rid themselves of anger and hatred.
> 'He abused me, he struck me, he overpowered me, he robbed me.'
> Those who do not indulge such thoughts rid themselves of anger and hatred.
>
> Dhammapada 3 & 4

---

[3] In looking at the Buddhist psychology of forgiveness, I have tried to make that clear and offered plenty of exercises: Towards the End of Forgiveness. Available as PDF under Dhamma Talks: www.satipanya.org.uk

12

THE CONSUMER IN US ALL

Have we noticed how consumerism has gradually become a worldwide religion, one that we have bought into?

We all know how advertisers create false needs: They suggest that what you are buying – a product, a service – is a bargain. Money well spent. They tell us it will make us especially happy. We will be so gratified – immediately!

The purchase will take such little effort. In fact, if all we do is tick this box, buy into this loan plan we won't even notice the money leaving our bank account. Plus we can win a prize!

At the end of December 2018, people in the UK owed £1. 625 trillion. The average total debt per household, including mortgages, was £59,261 that same month. Never mind the rest of the world!

This habit of greedily seeking a bargain has insinuated itself into our lives to the extent that the behaviour becomes automatic, seems natural, logical, is never questioned. Surely, it's been with us ever since bartering began.

But as a generalised attitude to life, it eats away at the good heart. For the consumer seeks to take as much as they can, while giving as little as possible. They are always on the lookout for that bargain.

While this is just another manifestation of our good friend, Greed, in its new logical and natural guise, it takes on an ethical air. It is confused with self-care: 'Greed is good.'

This attitude will affect our spiritual lives. Watch out for bargaining with or trying to profit from a spiritual practice.

Beware of looking for the pristine technique, the one really taught by the Buddha, the one to deliver the goods fast with the least possible effort. For instance, are we looking for that famous teacher everyone is talking about? What do we expect of the teacher? That they are actually going to get us to Nibbana? Do we expect them to be entertaining, exciting?

Can they give us the immediate gratification we want? All those vipassana knowledges – the ñāna– shouldn't they come quickly. 'I've read about them and they seem pretty straightforward to me! Why haven't I attained them yet? It can only be the teacher holding me up, or the method.'

'If I have to listen again to that boring talk with its same old jokes, I'll go mad.'

We need to ask ourselves if our spiritual practice is all about us. Remember dana – generosity? It is said that in giving we receive. Are we giving simply to receive?

I don't know where I got this quote:

> 'The One, or Oneness, as we might say in Zen, never tries to turn a profit from anything at all. It wouldn't even make sense. We, on the other hand, are always trying to turn a profit from every human exchange. We are always trying to get something – admiration, love, recognition, praise, acknowledgment, even just staying connected. Think how we manipulate and bargain and negotiate to turn a profit from every interaction. Much of this is subtle, unconscious habit. Even when we give, or serve, or love, or pay attention, we're trying to get something. Sometimes it's just to get back some of what we give.'

Unfortunately, the spiritual life asks almost exactly the opposite to our speedy, consuming society. It demands a long-term commitment, over lifetimes if we are open that. It demands dogged perseverance. Although highlights and wonders appear, they are merely short stops on the Path. The Path is a constant struggle against Mara, our unwholesome habits – the Five Hindrances, the Defilements and the subtle, unconscious Latent Tendencies that we don't know are there or we don't know how powerful they are until a situation springs them out of hiding.

Why were these the Buddha's last two words: Appamadena sampadetha – with diligence work hard? 'Strive diligently for your liberation!'

For more on this topic, read: Cutting Through Spiritual Materialism by Chogyam Trungpa Rinpoche – it is still a classic.

13

ISOLATION LONELINESS SOLITUDE

Feeling isolated is not the same as feeling lonely. The former comes from being out of touch with those whom we feel close or affiliated to. Loneliness, on the other hand, can be a very painful state, coming after the death of a loved one, the loss of a friend or when we move into a new area and don't know anyone.

I live at Satipanya, isolated from the Sangha, for example. As a monastic, I feel at home in the company of other monastics – of whatever creed. This is the same for anyone in the trades or professions. They all have guilds, unions or associations where they can mingle. In the same way we can feel isolated from our friends and families when we don't have enough or easy association with them, but we don't necessarily feel lonely. Family gatherings play a similar role for family members and without them they become isolated. But this is not to be confused with loneliness.

When we feel lonely, we remember those times we felt unloved, abandoned in childhood or young adulthood. Loneliness tells us we are dependent on someone to feel worthy, loved and wanted. Sitting quietly with these feelings that may arise for whatever reason can allow old buried and unresolved feelings to arise. And they usually centre around our belief that we are unlovable.

The heart longs to divulge its secret pain, but finds no one to trust. And in that vulnerability, touches on the fragile nature of its existence. Sitting with loneliness can open our eyes to our inner selves. It's a healing process. We need to wait until all feelings of loneliness disappear. What then arises?

Solitude is of a different order. It is often what we seek when we have had enough company, enough excitement. It's such a relief sometimes to be on our own. But this is poor solitude. It doesn't last very long. As soon as we have rested, we get fed up with ourselves and off we go into the helter-skelter of excitement seeking.

Solitude, at its true spiritual depth, is to find one's home within. As a Latin saying goes: Never less alone than when alone. This is the gift of a heart no longer in need of the other, a heart that is content.

I wonder if you can catch this solitude, an inner sense of a self-embracing all-one-ness, when you've sat in vipassana with a bout of loneliness and waited patiently for it to transform.

14

ENVY JEALOUSY APPRECIATIVE JOY

It's okay to say 'I envy you' because it can be a way of praising someone while showing that we'd like what they have. I know a monk who told me of his intention to retire as abbot. His news elicited in me a desire to reduce my teaching rota and spend more time on retreat and study. When I told him I envied him, I did not covet what he had, but instead experienced a spur to move in the direction he had taken. The problem with 'I envy you' comes when we covet what the other has and feel the pressure to 'keep up with the Joneses'. That's all to do with proving oneself to be equal or better than the other – a fool's game.

The antidote is to be grateful for what we have, to discern what we need rather than what we want. This allows for greater contentment. Not that we cannot better our situation, but let's not do it to compete with someone else.

Jealousy is a darker state. Here there is not only wanting what the other has, but also hating them for having it. This aversion can disguise itself as righteous criticism of the other. We can be dismissive of their achievements, their possessions. But there is a deeper comparison here, not of possessions, position and so on, but of selves. At worse the person nurtures a revenge for the belittlement they feel the other causes them – and yet they are oblivious to their own jealousy!

To accept that we are jealous is to realise we are defining ourselves as inferior – which is hard on self-esteem. Indeed, we can be in such denial that we project our jealousy onto them and fool ourselves into thinking they are jealous of us!

A blessing of the noting technique in our practice is that it can make us acknowledge this difficult attitude.

The antidote is appreciative or empathetic joy, mudita. First, as soon as we catch ourselves indulging our jealousy, we stop the thinking and imagining and see if we can feel the emotional value of the attitude in the body. If we can, if there's time, we stay there feeling and acknowledging its unwholesome and unpleasant feelings.

If there is no time or we cannot wait till the feelings exhaust themselves, we set them aside. Remember this is not suppressing them, but simply not identifying with or indulging them.

Then we praise the successes of the other. When we feel envious of what another has or achieves, we can celebrate their work, rejoice in their luck. When jealousy is aroused, we can praise not just what they have achieved, but their abilities and characters. And then wish them greater success – even through gritted teeth!

15

AWARENESS COMPASSION WISDOM

There has been a clear example of the difference between awareness of suffering and compassion. For so long Europeans have heard and seen on screens the suffering of refugees from the war torn Middle East or coming across the Mediterranean. Nothing really happened save on the Greek and Italian islands where these suffering people landed. It was only a photo in 2015 of the lifeless body of a drowned three-year-old Syrian boy that suddenly made the connection. Awareness of suffering became compassion – a heart connection that demands action. And some empathy did emerge to ease the crisis and not leave it all up to Turkey, Jordan, Italy and Greece – especially by Germany.

It is simple enough to acknowledge the distinction. Whenever we are aware of suffering of any kind, stay close to the heart. What do we feel? Is there fear or aversion? Maybe there is indifference or some other attitude that may bring up feelings of guilt and shame. After all we're supposed to be compassionate! All this, the negative reaction and the judgmental mind, have to be acknowledged and felt. It's not pleasant.

Then we have to put ourselves in the other's shoes. Or ask the question: 'If I was in that situation what would I hope people might do for me?' It is the central human relationship – do unto others as you would have them do unto you.

Consider the hardship of refugees. They've probably experienced bombings, lost family. They've escaped with little money – most given to traffickers for their passage to freedom – and little food. They undergo the dangerous sea voyage and arrive exhausted, shortly to be in despair about the future.

How would we feel to lose family, our home, our livelihood – our life as we knew it? It doesn't take long to conjure up sympathy. Sympathy is what we can feel through our imaginary efforts when we ourselves have not had such traumas. If we've some knowledge of loss, homelessness, penury, then empathy, a closer resonance in the heart, arises. Either way, they both lead to action.

But be careful not to overdo it! We can get caught up in the energy aroused by compassion. The bigger the group, the greater the energy. But then we find ourselves volunteering for work that is beyond our capability – physically, mentally, financially. It can begin to put strains on long established relationships, on work. In focusing too much on the suffering of one particular person or group, we become blind to the problems we may be causing for others, usually those near to us.

We can make sacrifices for ourselves, but not for others. If we can't carry people with us, we need to accept our limitations.

It may come down to either not helping others in an hour of need because those close to us or our work situation won't support this, or helping others with a detrimental effect on our relationship to those close to us or our work. We need to be clear about what we are prepared to lose.

Compassion without wisdom also leads to suffering.

16

APPAMĀDA : DILIGENT

Appamāda, one of the Buddha's favourite words, comes into his final exhortation: 'All compounded things arise and pass away. Strive diligently for your liberation.'

Although the Buddha mentions many virtues needed to stop unwholesome states arising and to develop wholesome ones, diligence can be understood to be one of the most important. In The Numerical Discourses of the Buddha, translated by Bhikkhu Bodhi, who prefers the word heedful, putting the accent more on care whereas diligent puts the accent on commitment.

I do not see even a single thing that so causes unarisen unwholesome qualities to arise and arisen wholesome qualities to decline as heedlessness. For one who is heedless, unarisen unwholesome qualities arise and arisen unwholesome qualities do not decline. AN 1.58

I do not see even a single thing that so causes unarisen wholesome qualities to arise and arisen unwholesome qualities to decline as heedfulness. For one who is heedful, unarisen wholesome qualities arise and arisen unwholesome qualities decline. AN 1.59

Synonyms for appamāda are: Hard-working, industrious, assiduous, heedful, meticulous, conscientious, thorough, attentive, careful, painstaking, persistent, vigilant, zealous.

We can sort them into three lists, the first to do with effort, the second with mindfulness and the third with care. You might organise them differently.

> Mindfulness: attentive, vigilant, heedful
> Care: careful, conscientious, meticulous, thorough, painstaking
> Effort: hard-working, industrious, assiduous, persistent, zealous

Each word brings a nuance to our reflection. In this way appamāda offers is a useful way to reflect on our actions. We ask ourselves: 'In the general how would I describe the way I think, say and do things?'

> Take each word and ask: 'Am I in general …?'
>
> Then for a daily reflection, ask: 'Have I been …?'
>
> Finally, after a task, ask: 'Was I …?'

Appamāda is a quality within right attitude in the Eightfold Path. If we consciously practise this attitude in the way we think, speak and act it will become an instilled habit.

Of course, this presumes that the intention and act arise out of wisdom, right understanding, for these are the same qualities you need to rob a bank!

Let's look at the antonym: lazy, sluggish, slothful, can't be bothered, do it tomorrow. That's what we have to see first of all, the underlying unwholesome tendency (anusaya) and the presenting defilement (kilesa). As ever, we recognise it, acknowledge it, feel it and stay with it a while if there's time. If not, park it, put it to one side without fear or aversion, refuse to be hijacked and raise appamāda.

17

PASSIVE AGGRESSION

When we are not getting what we want we can sometimes feel angry, upset, disappointed. Yet for one reason or another we won't accept the situation and work towards our goal. We feel such negativity that we can't talk calmly about the problem. We don't want to be openly angry either for fear of the other's reaction – they may be more powerful, the boss at work, for instance.

So we find ourselves in an unhappy situation, unable to do anything about it. We may choose to undermine the other, not realising this makes things worse. Unfortunately, it may be an habitual reaction, perhaps we aren't alert to our behaviour as an expression of anger, frustration. We are bewildered by the other getting so upset with us. We may not be aware that we are indulging in a form of bullying.

A common strategy is to ignore the person we are angry with. We may justify it ('she's impossible!'), but we want to avoid conflict and punish them at the same time. Consider how we feel when we are ignored.

Another ploy is to be late. We may give ourselves all sorts of excuses – had this to do and that, the mobile rang, just missed the bus, the train. When someone is late a lot of the time how do we feel? At meditation, what is our response when the same person repeatedly arrives a minute or two after time?

Perhaps we spitefully withdraw the usual things we do – sex, cooking, gardening, taking on responsibility not strictly ours at work and then not doing it without telling anyone. How do we react when someone does this to us?

What about doing something badly and then blaming everyone? In reality, we couldn't be bothered. And anyway we didn't like the way we were asked or 'why was I asked to do this'. How do we feel when we've asked someone to do something for us, they have agreed, but obviously done it in a slapdash way and left a sense of irritation in the air.

All such behaviours can be used at work to undermine the boss or the junior.

If we know we tend to use passive aggressive tactics, it is good to ask ourselves how that helps a situation. Surely we could find a time, no matter how difficult it may be, to be honest with the other. In truly intolerable situations, losing a friendship or work may be preferable to carrying on feeling angry, frustrated and miserable all the time.

If we're the target of passive aggression, what can we do? Often we have to wait for an appropriate time and place to talk to the person, undermine any fear they have of us; show them we are willing to accept that we may have behaved wrongly; that we are prepared to come to an arrangement. The worst we can do is to react with anger. If they're unaware of their passive aggression, they'll just deny it.

> Why are you sulking? I'm not sulking.
>
> Is there something wrong? No!
>
> I feel you are angry with me. Why would I be angry with you?
>
> You are late again. Everyone is late once in a while. Why are you so angry about it?
>
> You've done the job so poorly. Sorry! I know you would have done it better.

Our practice teaches us to keep in close contact with our feelings because they tell us how we are reacting. This can enable us to be honest with ourselves, to avoid acting passive aggressively – especially towards another who is acting the same way because that only worsens the situation and makes us feel bad.

I recently began getting strong passive aggressive signals from a family living nearby. Even the boy gave me dirty looks. I finally got the opportunity to talk to the wife and explained what I was experiencing. I asked her why it was happening, saying I was sure it was a misunderstanding. She denied the whole thing. I hoped to catch the husband and try another tack. Then something strange happened. I went out to the post box and they were coming down the road. I greeted them. They were both very welcoming. They went to the gate to see their two beautiful Shetland ponies and their foals. I joined them and the husband suddenly started a friendly conversation. I never did get to the bottom of it.

If all this strikes a bell, there's lots on the websites.[4]

---

[4] I found this very informative: http://www.counselling-directory.org.uk/passive-aggressive.html

18

RIGHT SPEECH

Of the three moral categories in the Eightfold Path – right speech, right action and right livelihood – the first is probably the hardest to keep. This is mainly because we are always talking if not to others then to ourselves. The only respite is sleep!

Right speech is expressed negatively in the Five Training Rules: Not to use wrong speech.

Wrong talk includes lies, slander, coarse language and useless talk. Lies, I mean real lies, we probably don't tell any more. But what about exaggerations? And to what end are we exaggerating. To puff ourselves up, to defend ourselves, even to belittle ourselves? And similarly towards the other.

Slander means telling someone about another's faults or misdemeanours, but it depends on the purpose. Is it to do them harm or is to warn someone? And there's 'A truth told with bad intent – Beats all the lies you can invent', said poet William Blake

Coarse language usually emerges from lust or anger, but can also be a bad habit. Ask what effect it has. Is it to be one of the boys or girls, a sort of bonding? Is that the company we want to keep?

Useless speech is simply talking for talking's sake – it does not include the usual social pleasantries. In the Discourses, we often read of someone visiting the Buddha where there were 'some exchanged greetings with him, and when the courteous and amiable talk was finished, sat down to one side'. M60.3

We find it difficult to be silent with another, even when we know them well. The other can feel uncomfortable if we don't speak. And so can we. So if we cannot keep silent, then at least let us guide the conversation to something mutually interesting.

The Buddha gives us pointers to use speech skilfully. Apart from the reverse of the above, he suggests that what is said is:

>Spoken at the right time: Often we have to choose when to say something especially if the other will find it difficult to hear.

>True: We have to remember that our words may not be heard as we intend them to be heard. We may have to check with the listener. In an interview, the teacher may repeat back to the meditator what they said to be sure they have heard properly.

>Spoken gently: Sometimes that might mean counting to 10.

>Beneficial: Of benefit to the other, or to ourselves, or to both of us.

>Spoken with the heart of loving-kindness.

What about not speaking when we ought to? Was it because we were afraid? Confused? Or is not talking a way we express our anger, spite, sourness?.

Then again, silence can speak volumes. It's tricky stuff!

In general, the route to Right Speech is pausing before we speak, glancing inward and knowing our mental state. If the heart is in a poor place, then come from the seat of wisdom.

Not easy!

19

EQUANIMITY

Equanimity is not a word you hear often. Initially, I didn't really know what it meant: Something about the balanced mind?

In the Buddha's teaching, it is arguably the most important of all virtues. By sitting on the bed of equanimity, the other virtues are less likely to be corrupted into their direct or subtle enemies. We're more likely to see things as they really are.

Every virtue has its opposite: love / hatred; generosity / greed; courage / cowardice. This holds for more subtle ones too: love / attachment; generosity / overly generous (detrimental to oneself or the other or both); courage / foolhardiness.

We expect equanimity of judges, that they won't get tangled up in lawyers' clever arguments. The baying crowd won't sway their intellectual clarity. Then there's the emotional heart. Judges are supposed to be impartial. They shouldn't be angry with the criminal and let that influence their sentencing. When summing up, guiding the jury and sentencing, they won't be fearful of possible reprisals from a guilty criminal. They come from the rule of law, not from a personal angle.

So it is with equanimity in ordinary daily life. Do we know our biases? Do we only read, listen and talk to those who have the same views? Do we take the position of 'I'm right' or more subtly 'we're right'? It always feels more 'righteous' when others agree with us.

In a quiet moment when we can talk to ourselves truthfully, what do we really think about politics, sexual identities, religion and other questions of our time? How do we really feel? Does the feeling square with thought? Are there hidden darknesses we have kept secret from ourselves? Little prejudices that our ideal sense of self has not really allowed to be accepted? 'If I thought that, it wouldn't be me.'

From the position of the Dhamma, often translated as the Law, the Truth, what ought we to think and feel? Do we have the humility to accept that?

We are equanimous when we come into any given situation without prejudice, fear, anger or preference.

Mmmm! Well, that's what we are aiming for.

20

SHAME

Shame gets a bad press, as though we shouldn't feel it at all: 'All shame is bad.'

It may come as a surprise then to learn that the Buddha regarded shame as a guardian of society and coupled it with guilt or fear of consequences.

We feel shame or its lesser form embarrassment when we've let ourselves down, especially in other people's eyes.

There is the delightful tale of Sir Walter Raleigh who, presumably as he bowed to the Queen Elizabeth, let out a great fart. He did not reappear at court for year or so. On his return, the Queen greeted him warmly, saying: 'We have forgot the fart.'

We are often more ashamed by social gaffes than by immoral behaviour. And I dare say if we get away with it, we have none at all.

Are we ashamed when we slander someone, no matter how slight? Or when we take the pen home from the office? Or exaggerate to the point of untruthfulness?

Some shame can be too delicate, for example an over-sensitive conscience. A small gaffe of calling someone by the wrong name keeps us up at night. We avoid society because of how we look. We freeze when we stand up in public (shyness often masquerades as shame). Counselling may be of benefit here.

Being aware of the feeling, recognising it as unwholesome and waiting for it to pass or do what we have to do anyway – this is vipassana in action.

In the Buddhadhamma, shame is always seen as unwholesome for it arises when we do or think something that belittles us. And yet without it and its companion, the guilty fear of consequences, what would stop us from criminal acts?

The desire not to suffer shame and guilt – that is wholesome.

So our task is to reflect on any thought, speech or action that we identify as unethical, harmful or insensitive and to acknowledge what shame or lack of it came up.

On feeling shame, we reflect on the harm done to see if its level is appropriate. We can talk to the person whom we imagine no longer respects us or holds us with the same regard, and correct or soften their view of us.

In acknowledging that our action is wrong, insensitive, inappropriate and yet there is no shame in it, again we need to reflect on why that is. Don't we care how people view us? What sort of self-respecting standards are we keeping if we can't care less about breaking them?

This is all to do with refining our moral conscience. It is about how we relate. The way we relate manifests our wisdom or lack of it.

21

GUILT

Like shame, the Buddha calls guilt a guardian of society. That guilty feeling tells us we're at fault, that we've done harm. This leads to the fear of consequences.

Existential guilt, suffered by some brought up in Abrahamic religions, is different. We have been told from an early age that we carry the sin of Adam and that we are essentially sinful.

This is not the fundamental reason for our transgressions. The Buddha said wrongdoing was secondary. The prior reason is non-culpable ignorance that causes us to fall into a delusion. We are essentially ignorant of the way things really are.

Because of this we commit errors based on acquisitiveness, aversion and fear. But paradoxically it is all done to make 'me' happy.

Even so this leads us into actions of thought, speech and deeds that harm us and others – and that is when we feel guilty.

Without guilt, without seeing that we are or were a cause of another's suffering and our own (how easy it is to blame others for our unhappiness), without being worried about the consequences, what would stop us doing harm?

As with all our unwholesome states guilt must be faced. In our meditation we open up to its tremors, the fear of being caught, the dread of consequence.

Maybe the guilt we feel is inappropriate. To be sleepless because you deliberately took a pen from the office, criticised your boss to someone whom you suspect might tell them or swatted a fly out of irritation may point to a guilt-ridden conscience, one full of scruples and qualms (the bugbear of the monastic life with all its 227 rules!) is a sign of imbalance. It can help to talk to a friend whose judgment you trust will give you a wiser perspective.

But when we feel no guilt or only a little after committing what society considers wrong tells us we need to contemplate the consequences of what we have done. I knew someone who, citing Marxist critique of a capitalist society, stole from a small bookshop regardless of the effect on the struggling owner.

When guilt is justifiable, however, we do need to turn into the feeling of guilt to see how painful it is. Really opening up to misery of that mental state is a departure for reflection: 'I would not be suffering this tormented heart, had I not behaved unskilfully.'

If we can put right what we did wrong with a gift, a simple apology, all well and good. But if an occasion for reconciliation does not arise, then reparation may be possible. Here is a rather extreme example. When a Hindu confessed to Ghandi he had murdered a Muslim child, Gandhi told him to find a Muslim orphan and bring him up as a Muslim.

Even if that is not possible, then we have no option but to sit with the guilt and express our remorse and sorrow within ourselves. And, of course, a fierce determination not to behave in a similar manner again.

When we experience the suffering of guilt, realise that it is the product of deluded unwholesome action, we are more able to forgive others who do harm, for they will also suffer the same.

Guilt, then, is also a first step towards compassion.

22

GRATITUDE GENEROSITY RENUNCIATION

Any talk the Buddha gave to lay people began with dana, generosity: 'Even a thief can be generous!'

We can be giving with our time and wealth. But for the act to be truly unselfish it has to be given without conditions.

A friend needs a lift, we help her out. If we now believe she can be called on when we are in need, then that is not generosity, it's a business contract. Such deals are fine, but don't confuse them with generosity.

We're out with someone and offer to buy the tea. If we get upset when the friend does not reciprocate, then ours was not unselfish. It was a business contract.

Any giving has to hurt a little. Donating £5 a month to a favoured charity may be hardly generous. How would £10 or £20 feel?

If a friend is taken to hospital, how long should your visit last? If your decision suits you more than the sick person, then it's not generosity. Because generosity puts the other first.

So let's be clear, generosity always – that is always – demands renunciation. We give up time and wealth for the other's benefit without recompense or refund. At all times, it hurts a little.

When we give up something, we relinquish a false dependency. Every time we surrender a little attachment, the self shrinks. It clutches for personal use only and out of fear of loss. Generosity releases the cramp.

This is its gift – releasing us from false needs and dependencies.

The question is, what motivates generosity in the first place. Compassion when we see suffering, of course. Expressions of love and joy too. But it is gratitude that bolsters our giving.

Spend a moment considering what we have received where payback was never sought: As a child (the Buddha reminded us that even if we carried our parents on our shoulders throughout our lives we could never repay them for the gift of life), support of family, education, healthcare, our culture – the Buddhadhamma.

The paradox is that the more we give and the greater the sacrifice, the deeper the sympathetic joy. But beyond even this, the virtuous circle twirls us towards our liberation.

23

EXCITEMENT BOREDOM CONTENTMENT

Confusing excitement with happiness – that's where the trouble starts. We can get excited about anything – trainspotting, juggling, tiddly-winks. What it is, is immaterial so long as it excites us. We can absorb quickly into that mental state and for that time it is, well, heaven. Some absorb into beautiful states through meditation and may mistake them for Nibbana. So long as we can be lifted into that state, all is well. But when the gratification wanes, disappointment sets in.

After a joyous meal or party with old friends or family, we agree to do it again. The second time doesn't have the same spark. Suggestions for yet another get-together are met with forced smiles and faint nods. Come the date, excuses abound.

But what if we have to repeat the same thing to the point where work that once was so interesting no longer is, or the breath in sitting is no longer the haven it once was. Aversion sets in, a type of restless dislike that moves towards listlessness and a feeling of meaninglessness. Then a deeper boredom sets in, a sense of wasted time. The driving search for something else kicks in: Fidgeting through websites, flicking through TV channels, scrolling though social media, the pursuit of biscuits. And can I observe the breath there instead of here? Better still let the mind live in its virtual reality.

And suddenly we find joy – so off we go again, indulging in a new passion: foraging for mushrooms or playing the Great Big War Game or saving the world from ecological disaster (some daydreams come from good intent). In sitting, scanning up and down the body. And the cycle cranks up once more.

Consumerism depends on this sort of intoxication. It's a religion that's onto a real winner because once hooked we are always chasing the new. New means good, means excitement. But how quickly we are bored and at the first tweak we start again to seek another pleasures here and there. Boredom is the underlying engine of consumerism.

However great the elation, boredom comes in equal measure. And the more thrills we indulge, the more we raise the bar, the greater the excitement has to be. Greed is utterly voracious. 'More' the adjective becomes 'More' the noun. We simply want More.

Should all the excitements lose their gloss, then boredom flowers into feelings of wasted time, of a vacuous lifestyle, then the loss of hope of ever enjoying life again arises – and that leads to apathy and despair. Endgame, of course. But for most of us, we can take boredoms as a warning.

The cure? Repetition with good intention. Re-establish why we are doing our job and do it for that reason. Raise a sense of care to be excellent and interest reappears.

The joy of living returns if we acknowledge that much of what we do is useless entertainment and we determine to spend time more usefully.

Practise renunciation. Let go of all that planning. What will we do this evening, this weekend, next month? Do something simple instead. Over a series of weekends, do the same walk, prepare the same simple meal. Draw the attention into the present doing and develop contentment: This is the way it is and it is okay.

Contentment is poison to boredom.

24

COURAGE FORTITUDE RESILIENCE

At least once in our lives, everything collapses around us – and it leaves us desperate. Maybe we've failed to get the qualifications for the work we've set our heart on. Or we've lost the job we love. Maybe a relationship we depend on has ended. Or someone close has died. Perhaps illness demands a radical change in our lives.

First comes shock and disbelief and, as reality penetrates, utter desolation.

This is a crucial moment, one where we can descend into the hell of depression, even suicide – or into purgatory where we begin the process of rehabilitation. What we experience in purgatory is equal to that of hell, except for the change in attitude: We have reinstated a reason for living.

This takes courage as our first task is to ask why the catastrophe has happened. The reasons may be beyond our control; The economy, perhaps, or the other has been unfaithful or, true to its nature, the body has fallen ill. In such cases, there is only acceptance along with a shift to the internal world to work with the emotional and mental reactions. And to explore potential.

But if overconfidence was at fault and mainly responsible for ending a relationship, for putting the body in danger, then a deep trawling of our attitudes is needed. This takes patience, fortitude and perseverance – resilience.

The situation may demand a change of direction in our lives. It may call for continuing as we were, but with a different attitude. It may mean a radical acceptance of a situation that cannot be altered.

Once we've made this decision, no matter how dimly we see the potential outcome, we are on the road to rehabilitation.

A spiritual awakening may coincide with this experience. For in our misery, we may question the purpose of life. Such collapses may also happen in our spiritual lives. In fact, I would say this has to happen to some degree. The world view we hold is, according to the Buddha, a delusion. When we confront that delusion, it is bound to cause a disruption. And that dis-location can be as painful as any mundane one.

We may have a sense of groundlessness and bewilderment, yet the inner conviction, no matter how dim, supported by the writings, experience and example of others, gives us the courage to commit and the determination to persist.

In the Buddha's own darkest hour when Mara generated in him the Great Doubt – Who am I after all to seek the end of suffering? – he had to ground himself. And the Earth Goddess rose to remind him that his task was not just for his own benefit but for the benefit of all. She told him he had perfected the virtue of generosity and so had the virtuous power to complete the task. Rooted to his seat beneath the Bodhi Tree, after six hours, came the insight into the end of all suffering, the direct experience of Nibbana.

There is an end to suffering, to all unsatisfactoriness. It is our only real destination.

25

ONE OF THE HINDRANCES IS SCEPTICAL DOUBT

Sceptical doubt stops us doing anything. First time on a diving board and we doubt we can do it. Fear is rationalising so we climb down.

We apply for a job we doubt we have the ability for – and the mind offers a rational argument for our fear of failure.

We doubt that the person we love can really love us, carbuncles and all, so we delay ... and delay for fear of rejection. And they find someone else.

Sometimes we have to make a leap of faith – made all the easier if we abandon the notion that life is a series of successes and failures. Instead we see it as an exploration – a series of 'trial and error'. Then we can jump. We can 'fail'. We can try again.

So it is with the Buddhadhamma.

We may have many doubts, in the teaching, the practice, the teacher but most often in ourselves. Many teachings may be difficult for us: Not-self, karma and rebirth, transcendence and Nibbana, no personal, all-loving God.

If we allow these doubts to overwhelm us, we will stop the practice, commit spiritual suicide! Yet the Buddha does ask us to have doubt – an honest doubt. It is the wonder of the philosopher.

This curiosity will overcome the inevitable fears we'll meet as we explore our unknown inner territory. For the Buddha did not ask us to believe what he said, but to question it. The process he has given us to investigate is vipassana.

We are asked to question not intellectually, but experientially. We must discover for ourselves if his teachings are true for us.

This very exploration is the course of liberation for it dissolves our delusions, demanding that we overcome our sceptical doubts.

The latter often arise when we are asked to abandon our cherished certainties. But do we know if these certainties are true from our own experience? Or are they beliefs we have unquestionably accepted on the word of others, of family tradition, of culture?

Can we remain in that place of 'don't know', 'not sure'?

After all, why come to a conclusion at all if we don't know whether it is true – or not – by our own personal experience?

26

FEAR

Have you ever allowed yourself to feel fear? I don't mean a fearful or anxious state but the raw, intimate emotion? The simple sensation of it? Not sitting by the fire, but jumping into it?

Wherever a self / a 'me' is, ready to defend, there will be fear. Because the self, that sense of me, that I am someone, knows it cannot exist for ever and is going to die. Fear of death is the mother of all fears.

Yet who would want to sit still in the midst of that experience – the cold agitation, suffocated breath, debilitating weakness, exploding heartbeat, nausea? Surely we can do something about it?

Yes we can! We turn to social media, nothing like talking to others about the weather, the tennis, Brexit, to get away from fear. Nothing like eating or drinking. Alcohol is such a salve.

Or perhaps the primal fear has morphed into other fears: Fear of loneliness or anger or love or spiders. I say morphed, but this is another way of guarding ourselves. To attach a fear to something is more bearable than the fear of death, annihilation, total loss.

To guard ourselves well, we need to control. The more we control, the more we feel safe so we can guard what we have and fend off attacks real or imaginary.

Then there's anger. Anger empowers us: 'Where there is fear, I shall fight.' Anger feels good and frightens others. It protects 'me' from my fear. And I love to dominate and see the fear in others.

But in the worst-case scenario we run, hide, seek seclusion. What about shopping, jogging ... sex?

Have you uncovered your strategies?

The Buddha did not say the path was easy. He said it was gradual and against the stream.

With every fear that arises we receive a chance to sense the raw emotional material. Slowly we become accustomed. And the more familiar we are with those emotional sensations the more we lose our fear of them.

We realise it is the deluded heart that goads the mind into horror scenarios. And as our fear of fear subsides, we begin to see the possibility of fearlessness. In losing our fear of fear, what could possibly frighten us?

And since fear is the measure of our self-delusion, so the sense of self diminishes until such time as the wrong view of self, the belief that sense of self is substantial and essential, is completely cut asunder.

While the materials of fear dissolve, the barriers of defense weaken. The once embattled heart begins to embrace.

Then we understand how we might suffer for another – die for another.

27

PATIENCE

The Latin pati (to suffer) is the root of the word patience. Other words derive from it too – patience, a patient, passion. But in the sense of the virtue, patience means to bear with the unpleasant, the unpleasing, with suffering.

It harbours qualities the Buddha would have included: Forbearance, tolerance, restraint, self-restraint, resignation, stoicism, fortitude, sufferance, endurance.

The scriptural Pali word khanti is probably best translated as patient endurance, but like all virtues has a wide coverage – everything from minor irritants to major physical pain and psychological torment.

What attitudes might foster the patience that the Buddha calls the greatest of all ascetic virtues?

When it comes to momentary situations having awareness of our irritation arising allows us to resist indulging it. We may have to overlay it with good will for it does not pass on the acknowledging of it. If we find ourselves in conversation with someone who has contrary views, we are aware of our anger bubbling up and positively put our attention towards the attitude of careful, respectful listening.

Maybe we can do nothing about a situation and instead of getting into conflict, it would be wiser to develop patient forbearance. It may be great pain with no available palliative or a neighbour with penetrating music or a bullying boss. Accepting a situation is not being resigned to it, but to continuously seek a solution. And when no solution can be seen, we have no option but to learn to live with it. Here is an opportunity to practice affectionate awareness. Difficult as it may be, it is an awareness that also engages the heart into a form of kindliness or caring.

So how much patience should we have?

The Buddha sets the bar high!

> 'Bhikkhus, even if bandits were to sever you savagely, limb by limb, with a two-handled saw, he who gave rise to a mind of hate towards them would not be carrying out my teaching.
>
> 'Instead we should abide compassionate for their welfare, with a mind of loving-kindness, without inner hate.'
> Bhikkhu Bodhi The Discourse of the Simile of the Saw. MN21

To do this, it would help to recognise in the other their Buddha nature and that they like us are also seeking happiness, no matter how deluded it may be.

28

JUDGMENTAL OR JUDICIOUS?

Judging, with all the confusion around it, gets bad press in the practice. We're supposed to note it day and night as 'judging, judging'. But if we don't judge, how do we come to decisions? How do we know what's skilful or unskilful? In fact the very acknowledgement that we are judging is a judgment.

We note 'judging, judging' when we hear ourselves criticising. And we love to criticise because it makes us feel grander than others and better about ourselves. When turned towards ourselves, what sweet wounding it is to beat ourselves up for we know we deserve it!

These injuries rise out of the usual suspects – selfishness, hatred and fear in all their varied forms. And the delusion is that it is for the victim's good. And the fact is, the truth of the judging may be so. If we perceive someone as deceitful, we may balk at the judgment. But they may very well practise deceitfulness. For fear of judging, we do not guard ourselves against their deceitfulness. Surely this is folly.

If I judge myself as lazy – which I do– I might dismiss that as hateful self-judgment. But I am lazy, sometimes.

In civic life, when it is time to vote we have to judge the party we will support. If we call it judging, we will find it difficult to come to a decision – if at all.

So where does this judging go awry? Can we distinguish between judicious and being judgmental? Surely this is where the confusion lies. To be judgmental is to judge the person rather than the act, the politician and party rather than the policy. To come from a position of pride, aversion and so on.

The judgmental is a product of conceit. Better than, worse than or equal to. It's always about me and the other. Even when it's about me only, it presumes the standard of the other.

The old adage hate the deed not the doer makes it sound easy. But if I was deceived by that person and to separate the deceit from the person is no easy thing.

One way, perhaps, is to phrase what has happened in terms of what was done or received and how we were affected by it.

'I was told to come to a party at 10 Baker Street. I found there was no such place. It was a cruel joke at my expense. I feel hurt, vengeful. I shall wait till equanimity arises and decide what to do then. But for sure I won't be deceived again. I shall double check.'

As I said, no easy thing but try we must.

In our meditation, it shouldn't mean that we stop noting judging, more that we clearly see it is 'judging, judging' and that's okay. When we discern 'judgmental, judgmental', then we should note that and know it to be unskilful. The distinction is difficult to see, but unless we make it we will cause unnecessary suffering for ourselves.

29

OVERCOMING THE DISTORTIONS OF GENEROSITY

The self manifests as conceit and conceit is expressed in comparison: I am either better or worse or equal to you.

When it comes to generosity, the conceit 'I am better' is interpreted as 'I am truly a generous person'. Whereas 'worse' is critical: You should have given more, spent more time, listened more openly. 'Equal to' masquerades as humble: I'm only doing what others do. Here, 'others' stands for the likeminded, definitely not the stingy others.

Before we give our time or wealth, we stop and acknowledge that this is also an opportunity for the self to develop a lot of pride. We can undermine this by holding the clear intention to give for the benefit of another without return. We do this more easily when we donate to charities that we support but have no contact with, for example a homeless charity. But it gets tricky when we are part of an organisation or family or friendship group. We will know how pure our giving was when we don't get a return because it will show itself as hurt and the intention not to give again.

Part of the do-gooder profile is the desire for return in the form of praise or generous response. They are the people who want to help you – whether or not you want it. In general, they tell rather than ask you what you need and then they give it to you. When not appreciated or perhaps rebuked, they are mortally offended: 'I was only trying to help!' We all fall into this trap from time to time. To undermine this tendency, ask the person what they need or listen carefully to what it is they are asking for. No problem suggesting something else, but let them make the decision.

Then there is entitlement – a subtle corruption. Having done so much, surely they won't mind if I take a pen, bill them for a meal and take some cash. After all I don't feel I am appreciated enough. This can be the first step to fraud.

And how upset we can be with another's lack of generosity. That arises out of 'I am such a generous person!' Of course, a person can be stingy, a miser. But it's up to them to discover the joy in giving. It doesn't help to criticise them. How easily our joy in giving can give rise to conceit.

How do we develop the joy in giving? By giving! But giving with clear intention, aware of any defilements arising, not entertaining them and so disempowering them until they fade away.

30

WHAT VALUES GOVERN OUR LIVES?

What are our values and how do we rate them in importance?

How much of our lives is motivated by success in other people's eyes? If this is where most of our energy goes, it will be given to gaining such totems of success as power, riches and fame.

When the self is involved in self-aggrandisement, only caring for or overly caring for one's social image, then we are in conflict with the world, for our aim is to accumulate whether it be power, riches or kudos. This puts us into areas where others are seeking the same. Conflict, whatever the intensity, hardens the heart because it has no concern for the rival. When generalised, this loss of empathy leads to indifferent attitudes towards such areas as human rights: 'Just as I have to fight for my gains, so should you!'; and nature: 'I'll stop plundering the earth when everyone else stops.'

Furthermore, in fighting for what we want in order to look good, we have to learn the tricks of winning such as manipulation, deceit and making sure we know how to take advantage of hierarchy.

This thrusts us into judgmental mode, constantly rating others, measuring ourselves against others, culminating in pride, envy, jealousy and outright hatred.

The problem, however, does not lie in power, riches, fame or any other signal of celebrity success. If we want to change the world for the better, influence or power is required. If we happen to have a good commercial idea or a special international skill, money flows towards us.

We may have talent that lots of people want to enjoy. We would be poorer society without good politicians (beware the cynic!), entrepreneurs and artists.

The problem as always is how we relate to this. How do we gain our self-worth without these negative consequences? The answer is to make sure we are coming from the right place: right understanding and right attitude.

An easy way to recognise when we are acting out of wrong understanding and attitude is by becoming aware of our negative and conceited thoughts and any other unwholesome reactions.

It's when we don't 'feel appreciated', 'praised enough', 'valued'. When people don't 'show the respect owed to us' and so on.

This is why the Buddha asks us to reflect wisely.

For optimum spiritual results, let's imbue what we do with the virtues of generosity, service, respect for others, appreciation of others' work, integrity, loyalty – the list goes on.

31

VALUES IN MINE OWN EYES

Generally speaking, a part of us seeks our values dependent on what society calls success. This may make us feel good about ourselves, but it is dependent on the approval of others. But another part of us is self-accepting.

The more self-accepting we are, the less we feel the need for praise from others. So we don't care so much for the trappings of 'success'. Our work in itself and our lifestyle are self-satisfying.

Because we are not so caught up in how we look in others' eyes, we can open up to them. We relate not from a position of 'What should you do for me to make me feel good?' or 'What should I do to make you think highly of me, so I can feel good about myself?', but 'What can I do for you?', 'What can we share?' We will find ourselves more interested in the other as other, not a means.

When this is generalised, we begin to care about the environment, about human right issues, about other people's sufferings.

Because we don't seek praise, because self-acceptance brings joy-in-oneself, we can admire others and rejoice in their success.

Because we don't need friends for our psychological well-being, we can enter into generous friendships.

Because our relationship with our family is based on love rather than psychological need, we care for them without a feeling of imposed obligation or demand – even should they be demanding or try to make us feel obliged.

We are willing to put ourselves out to do what we can for the sick and elderly. We don't experience them as a burden.

When this is generalised, we may find ourselves more involved in society as a whole, perhaps in some charity work.

Because we don't set our values by the standards of others, we can be more objective about social standards and we find we can form values that are true to ourselves. They need not necessarily be any different, but they arise from within us. We don't impose them on ourselves because we want the admiration of others.

How to develop these qualities?

As usual, we have to be aware of our motivations which by now may be so habitual that they are subliminal. We are not always aware of them. It is through our reaction that we identify our original motivation. Should we notice any painful or unwholesome reaction, we can stop and reflect, and thereby see any unwholesome aspect of our original motivation.

Why are we upset when someone doesn't say thank you? Why do we feel so belittled when someone criticises us? Why do we feel bored or averse to what we are doing when we were once thoroughly interested and engaged?

Once aware of unwholesome attitudes, we can make sure that when we do something similar or meet the same person again, we approach them with the right motivation.

As always, the trick is mindfulness and wise reflection – and right intention.

SEEKING TRUE HAPPINESS

1
NOT AN EMOTION

What do we mean when we say we're happy? And however we define happiness, are we referring to a mood or an emotion?

A mood would be a present disposition that stays for a while. It may be caused by good fortune, for instance a distant relative dies and unexpectedly leaves us money. Or perhaps something we have been striving or hoping for has materialised: We applied for a job and succeeded.

An emotion is more transient. To cheer ourselves up, we take a walk in the country, visit a pub (for tea, of course!) or local park where they serve teacake and decent coffee. We feel good so we visit someone. We want to do something exciting and take flying lessons.

But the great flaw in this is that it cannot be maintained. By nature it's transient, impermanent and therefore unreliable.

And worse when I say 'I' am happy, that is how I am defining myself. So when 'I' am not happy, I start wondering why, blaming myself or others or society for my inability to be so.

I may believe that feeling happy is how I, how everyone ought to be. That it's natural. That being unhappy is unnatural. Suddenly it's writ large in national declarations and international treaties – the 'pursuit of human happiness'. It's become a 'right'!

Unfortunately, this just adds more striving with the potential for more frustration. The happier we try to be, the more unhappy we seem to get.

Happy moods and emotions are alright in themselves, but will they yield the substantial happiness our hearts seek?

If we can appreciate these transient experiences and don't try to recreate or better them, they will stand on their own as times to be delighted in.

The ability to say goodbye to a happy mood or emotion is to liberate ourselves from a psychological dependency.

When there is no psychological need for such states, we will enjoy them more. This is the meaning of non-attachment.

2

RELATIONSHIPS

Our lives are spent mainly with others, doing things together. If we can rate our happiness by our relationships perhaps we are on a surer footing.

When people enter a relationship, it always has a purpose beyond present gratification. It has a long-term aim. It may be a simple friendship – friends who meet to shop, to walk, to talk. It may form a partnership to set up a business or a charity. It may be a small enterprise or getting together to help someone.

Other relationships may deepen into longer term commitments such as partners and spouses, parents and guardians of children. These are never 'happy' from start to finish. After the first flush of joy, we start working to 'make it work'. At times difficulties emerge as we find the other has different ideas, different aims. Two out of three marriages fail. This could be judged as a measure of a broken society but given how difficult it is for individuals to be together, we should instead marvel that so many become lifelong.

Working with the other through tricky patches deepens a relationship, makes them more nourishing.

The Buddha tells us that we can do things that are good for ourselves or good for others and sometimes good both for ourselves and others.

On a visit to a small group of three monks, the Buddha asked the head monk how it was they lived so peacefully with each other. Venerable Kassapa replied that every morning he said to himself: 'What if I put aside what I want to do and do what the others want to do?'

We can see the wisdom in this approach. It allows us to loosen our grip on tightly held plans and ideas and allows the other to feel free to express theirs. Of course, for this to work all involved must have the same attitude.

The Arahat offers us this wonderful and skilful act of generous love, to put aside what we want to do until we establish what the other/s wish themselves.

Even at times when we have to agree to differ, this attitude supports co-operation and undermines resentment.

3

BEING GOOD VERSUS BEING GOOD AT

It seems obituaries have changed. Where once they described a person's qualities with examples, they now mention only what the person did. Achievements rate the person rather than character. As a result we come to believe that the famous, the rich and the powerful in our world are necessarily good people. Yet we know today's culture favours the bully, the callous entrepreneur, those who can muscle their way to the top.

Like it or not, this will influence how we think about ourselves. But to judge ourselves by our achievements, the work we do, our status, leaves few of us satisfied. We are into the game of comparison that leads to great effort to 'prove oneself'. This, in turn, leads to envy and jealousy of others. So we may end up being successful in the eyes of the world, but our hearts will be in turmoil.

If our hearts are polluted with the negativity of aggressive competitiveness or keeping up with the Joneses, this cannot be conducive to happiness, to an inner sense of worthiness. We never feel ourselves to be quite good enough.

In the Discourse on Blessings, the Mangala Sutta, as well as such social qualities such as being 'well educated and skilled, a highly trained discipline', the Buddha lists such qualities as generosity, ethical conduct, blameless actions, reverence, humility, contentment, gratitude, patience, gentleness, self-discipline... these are the Highest Blessings.

> Whose mind does not flutter by contact with worldly contingencies, theirs is sorrowless, stainless and secure. Dhammapada – Collection of Sayings

It's not that what we do doesn't matter. Far from it. What we do is an expression of our attitudes and the intentions that arise out of them.

If we put the accent on our attitude and intention, making sure they are wholesome, and then act, that deed will enhance our feeling of goodness. Otherwise no matter how well it is done, it will carry negative undertones.

If a person's action is skilful yet they carry a negative attitude, they may well be chosen to do the jobs, but they won't make many friends.

So if we want to feel good about ourselves – and want people to feel good about us – all we need do is get the attitude right.

Next time you are doing something whether for yourself, for a friend or at work, just stop before you do and ask yourself: 'What is the underlying attitude that is accompanying the work?' If it's negative, park it, bring a wholesome attitude into your heart. If it feels false, that's okay. It can take a while for the emotional heart to catch up with Right Attitude. Then do the work.

Hum Ella Fitzgerald's old song – T'ain't what you do, it's the way that you do it.

Right Attitude leads to Right Intention leads to Right Action leads to a feeling of goodness within – another form of happiness.

4
WHAT'S WRONG WITH A BIT OF ATTACHMENT?

Attachment is one of those hackneyed words that crop up regularly in Buddhist literature. The previous term was 'detached', but that sounded really hard and cold so now you will read 'non-attached'. The word being referred to is taṇha, usually translated as 'clinging'. It all refers to a type of relationship we have with the world and our experience of it through the senses and the mind and our relationship to those experiences.

We always have to remember that the Buddha's teaching is concerned only with suffering and unsatisfactoriness and the end of it – which is happiness. So we could say the Dhamma is all about attaining happiness. But that would be wrong. Indeed before his liberation from suffering that's what the Buddha was trying to do, either through ecstatic mental states or self-mortification.

But the fact of the matter is that happiness is always there. It simply needs to be uncovered. That thick sticky layer of attachment has to go and lo and betide, we have joy – it has been there all the time.

Happiness here refers to quiet joy, resonating compassion, warm love or sublime equanimity. For it to emerge from beneath the suffering and unsatisfactoriness of life all we have to do is drop the attachment. Easier said than done, of course. But once we realise it is the cause of suffering we will do it. Thus the Buddha's Second Noble Truth: The cause of suffering and unsatisfactoriness is taṇha – unwholesome desire, thirst.

Attachments make us believe that our happiness depends on something or someone. We cling to and defend them against loss. While we are indulging ourselves, there's no problem. It's a sensual Nibbana. Consider how we 'lose ourselves' in a film, a hobby, our work, in food, sex and romantic love.

But what happens when we can't get what we want? Is there not frustration and grief should we lose our delight? And an abiding anxiety of possible loss, the fear of it being taken away by someone or something? We experience the compulsive need. Our overbearing habit demands gratification – we are truly enslaved. When we inevitably get bored and fed up with it, off we go in search of another excitement. If greed fuels the consumerist society, escape from boredom is the unacknowledged accelerator.

So to rid ourselves of this suffering we must first contemplate these facts till they really sink in. Even when they have, keep contemplating them.

At the beginning and end of every delightful experience, acknowledge it has arisen and passed away and will never return. It is more dead than Monty Python's parrot.

Finally, the Buddha advises us to develop the attitude of 'no preference'.

'How do you like your tea?'

'As it comes.'

5

SACRIFICE: THE MORE WE GIVE THE GREATER THE RETURN

Sacrifice comes from two Latin words: sacer meaning sacred, and facere, to make. Sacrifices to a god aim to propitiate the deity or ask a favour. In the Buddha's day, the king's sacrifice involved huge ritual slaughter of horses and cattle. Abraham's offering of his son softened the harsh desert God. Christ, who gave his life to benefit all humankind, is said to be the 'blood of the lamb'. To offer something we treasure for a higher cause is what we mean by sacrifice. It is the point where generosity demands great courage and conviction: 'No greater gift has man than to offer his life for another.'

Arahats, those who are fully liberated, are said to engender an inestimable field of merit. The power of their goodness is limitless. This is the meaning of puñña, merit or goodness power. The simple fact that they have arrived at that station of non-suffering, Nibbana, makes real the aim for all. Once Everest was conquered, it was then climbable. To become fully liberated we have to relinquish everything – eventually – and we are asked to do that on a promise. We've no idea of the outcome. We trust on hearsay. Our confidence may grow as the path becomes clearer through our practice, but in the end it is always going to be a leap of faith. We trust that sacrificing everything we treasure will yield a boundless return.

Few have the qualities it takes to give up everything immediately as did the Bodhisatta[5] when he left home. This Great Renunciation is so called because he gave up the whole of his family and social life to follow his personal quest. At the point of the Great Doubt, as it is put metaphorically, Mara the Evil One approached and asked him who he thought he was to seek such a goal as full liberation. When the Bodhisatta called on the Earth Goddess to witness his right, she says it was the Parami, the Perfection of Generosity, that permitted him to seek full liberation. Renunciation had become sacrifice and he was no longer acting for himself but for all humankind.

So let's start small. The world has so many causes that we can surrender something for, for instance all the spiritual charities that aim to heal our deepest dis-ease, social charities to alleviate suffering, those that try to ease the enormous suffering that our greed causes animals. And Mother Earth: What will we sacrifice for her?

Renouncing what we really treasure – wealth, time – is hard. Even our present situation might call upon us: Parents make sacrifices for their children; the children care for ageing parents. These too are paths to liberation.

Every time we yield to the demand for sacrifice we prepare ourselves for the greatest of all sacrifices: Releasing any hope of achieving lasting happiness in the sensual world. Only when we have accomplished this can the greater happiness arrive. Little by little …

There's a saying in Italian 'Chi va piano, va sano e va lontano': Who goes slowly, fares healthily and far.

---

[5] Bodhisatta in Theravada Buddhism is someone who determines to become a fully self-enlightened Buddha. Sri Lanka is said to have four such monks at this present time.

6

HOW WE LIVE, NOT WHAT WE BELIEVE

The Buddha warned his followers not to get caught up in the 'debates' that were popular in his day. Every full moon, in the bright glow of the cool tropical evening, people gathered at the shrines to hear religious teachers.

Their views conflicted. There were materialist annihilationists, much as today's atheists, and eternalists, similar to present day 'believers'.

Talking about speculative beliefs, whether the materialist atheist reducing everything to chemicals or the religionist belief in life everlasting, he advised against getting caught up in 'a thicket of views, a wilderness of views, a contortion of views, a vacillation of views, a fetter of views.' M.2.8

The religion versus science debates tend to be about provable facts. Neurobiologists say that because certain parts of the brain light up and certain chemicals function as we experience emotions, these are therefore emotions. But no one experiences emotions as electro-chemical happenings. Believers talk of a soul, a subtle body, the mind-made body. Only those who have experienced that can be sure of it – how then can they prove it?

If religion is about beliefs, stated facts, then all we will do is repeat the well-worn arguments of 'experts'.

In the Sutta Nipata, an early collection of the Buddha's sayings, he is quoted:

> The one who is full of rigid views, puffed up with pride and arrogance,
> who deems himself "perfect" [expert], becomes anointed in his own opinion...
> SN IV.12.12

When I became interested in Buddhism, I wasn't in search of a belief, but of a methodology that would help me out of the hole I'd got myself into. What was said, of course, made sense. But it was what I 'did' that led me to commit myself to Buddhadhamma. Such questions about rebirth and Nibbana weren't important to me. I left them to stew. Maybe in time I'd find out. What mattered was how the practice of meditation and moment-to-moment mindfulness was revolutionising my life. And this of course meant to understand how I was creating my own suffering.

The Buddha eschews philosophical or metaphysical questions. He's not concerned about why we suffer. Darwin's theory of evolution would have held little interest for him. Does it make life more meaningful knowing we are biologically descended from early mammals? Or knowing that our psychology is based on early human experience as hunter gatherers?

Religion is about how we live and depends on our understanding. Our actions give this understanding an experiential meaningfulness. Knowing all about mountain climbing is one thing – actually climbing a mountain is something else.

So we ask ourselves: What am I doing that is making my life more meaningful?

What makes it more meaningless?

7

TOWARDS THE GREATEST HAPPINESS

Very occasionally when I talk to someone about the Buddha's teaching and how it's all about bringing an end to suffering, they will say: 'But I am happy!' What they don't see is that their happiness is dependent on conditions and circumstance.

A student once said to me when we were talking about spiritual happiness that he got his all from music. I regret now not asking him: 'What happens if you go deaf?'

The Buddha points to Nibbana or Nirvana in Sanskrit: A way of being that involves a happiness independent of condition or circumstance. We are in its presence or vicinity, he says, when we are mindful. In other words, Nibbana is staring us in the face but we don't see it.

This is the importance of vipassana practice. Every time we sit in meditation in this way, we make an object of everything we are experiencing. This means the locus of the self, that self-awareness, feels itself to be other than what it is experiencing.

If it is separate from what it is experiencing in meditation then it must be independent of the sensations and feelings in the body, the emotions and moods of the heart, and the thoughts and images that pop into the mind.

When we are hovering this way amid the all, all that we are experiencing, what is it like? This is something we can reflect on within and at the end of a sitting.

We might answer: 'So what? It's not pleasant or unpleasant. It's not exciting in any way. It's dull. In fact I don't want to be like this all the time. I want to have fun!'

These thoughts belong to Mara the Enticer. This is our delusion in action. The kaleidoscopic pleasures of the sensory world still bewitch us. We don't see the danger of it and the consequent suffering of attachment and indulgence.

To wean ourselves off the world's intoxication, we need to develop a taste for stillness, peacefulness, silence.

In the country, nature is the great teacher; in the city, we need to make do. Sit by the window and watch the clouds or take a walk at a quiet hour in the park or even down a road. Or sit in position for no other reason than to allow the sensations of the breath to calm, to develop our taste for serene stillness.

When that loses its flavour, we shall naturally seek the greater happiness – Nibbana.

RELATIONSHIPS

1

CULTIVATING PATIENCE:

Relatives Friends Acquaintances Spiritual Companions

Our friendships rarely collapse in a moment. It takes time for the rot to creep in.

Recall a friendship that fell away or worse, be it a close relative, friend, acquaintance or spiritual companion. What were the initial strains? Where did the antagonism begin? Was there full awareness of it then or had it mushroomed unexpectedly into an argument? After the argument was there an attempt at reconciliation? Was that really heartfelt or a patch through which in time the sore began again to fester.

Had we put ourselves out for someone who did not return the favour when we needed it? Or was it us who had not come to their aid?

Had they spoken a sharp word, a judgment, that we took in good part? But they kept doing it, snide remarks that finally got under the skin. Or were we oblivious that our sarcasm was actually hurting because they laughed?

Was it a growing clash of opinions where agreeing to differ helped, but then the relationship got edgy until excuses were made and meetings stopped?

Was there envy over time that created an aversion towards the person and became jealousy? Were we aware it was jealousy and not a matter of going off them? Or were they jealous of us and we knew it, but didn't know how to work with it?

Did a friend overstep a boundary, become too familiar, make presumptions? How did we react? Were we brusque, angry? Or did we suddenly find ourselves told off?

Your spiritual teacher, did you have a bad time with them? Do you still blame them? If you took the role of guiding someone, were you truthful about the role you played in the break-up?

Contemplating lost friendships is important for we are creatures of habit and tend to make the same mistakes over and over until we wake up.

Once we recognise the mechanisms within that undermine friendship, whether our own characteristics or our reaction to such characteristics in others, we can become aware of the first signs and train ourselves to stop – even in mid-sentence – and establish the appropriate attitude of goodwill.

2

FOUNTAINS OF JOY:

Contemplating Relatives Friends Acquaintances Spiritual Companions

How varied our relationships are! How we change in the presence of others according to the circumstance and its demands. Accepting the limitation of certain relationships is a cause for joy.

Relatives can be difficult. Often family history has to be contended with. Just sharing genes doesn't mean we will get on. So many other factors are there. But a shared history may add significant depth to a relationship with any family member. I was surprised how close I felt to a cousin of mine dying from pulmonary embolism even though we had hardly seen each other since childhood. The closer the relative – parents and siblings as opposed to cousins– the deeper our commitment to their well-being can be.

Friends, from close lifelong companions to social, political, work-related, hobby co-enthusiasts and so on – all fill important roles in our lives. They help us develop our personalities and characters as we meld with their varied personalities and characters in the process of sharing the interests that drive us.

On the outer reaches, we find acquaintances some of whom might one day become really important in our lives.

But spiritual friendship is to be most treasured and celebrated for it helps us to realise our life's most profound goals.

Ananda, the Buddha's companion for the last 20 years of his life, often had only partial understanding. One day, he opined that good friendship, good companionship, good comradeship was half the spiritual life. Good here does not contain an obligation to like these friends and comrades – this is the liberating quality of a spiritual friend!

No, no, the Buddha tells him, it is the entirety of the spiritual life. If we have good friendship, good companionship, good comradeship, then we can expect to cultivate the Eightfold Path because of that support. (SN 45: 2)

How important is that!

So after each meeting a relative, a friend, an acquaintance or a spiritual companion, pause for a moment, appreciate the treasure, allow gratitude to arise and savour the joy.

3

INTIMATE RELATIONSHIPS: EROTIC AND ROMANTIC LOVE

The erotic is truly pleasurable. The fleshly pleasures – eating, drinking, sex, swimming – have a palpable groundedness in a way that mental states do not. So much so that the erotic can be isolated from romantic feelings and love. It is choosy and wants only what conventionally conforms to physical beauty or as near as possible without generating disgust. It becomes self-seeking thus objectifying the other to gratify its lust. Lust is sexual greed and like greed consumes the other or wishes to be consumed. The other is commodified. This is the perspective from which obsession and pornography emerge. When mixed with darker motives sexual crime may occur, some of which sinks into insanity.

Romance is the eroticism of the heart, the touching of two personalities. It is equally choosy, but unlike the regretted brevity of sexual activity, the flight of romantic feelings can tinge days with kaleidoscopic delight. To be in the beloved's company, even bringing them to mind, catapults the lover into the seventh heaven. And such is its sweetness that it too becomes a self-seeking aim. Again the other becomes something to be consumed in or by so blinding us to the beloved's fuller personality which, when it peeks through the gossamer veil, punctures and often utterly deflates the passionate ardour. If unrequited, it can become vengeful, giving rise to crimes of passion or despair or suicide.

Love roots itself in the other's personhood, their humanity and essence in all its fullness. It reaches beyond the pleasurable or the delightful to a commitment that may demand sacrifice: For better and for worse, for richer and for poorer, in health and in sickness. Nor has it any time restriction. To love and cherish till death do us part. Time passing is not important, only time present. So no matter what the relationship – girlfriend, boyfriend, partner or spouse – it is a renewed commitment from moment to moment. Difficult!

Only when both are embedded in love can the erotic and romantic play their roles of fulfilling at times the whole intimate relationship with physical pleasure and heart's delight.

So it doesn't matter what sort of intimate relationship we are in – boyfriend, girlfriend, partner or spouse so long as there is committed love.

4
CELIBACY

Some are born celibate, some have celibacy thrust upon them and some grow into celibacy, to coin Churchill's aphorism on greatness. In more religious times and even now in Buddhist countries, a woman may boast she is still a virgin. And a man with no sexual encounter is considered no less a man when he joins the Sangha as a child or young teenager.

How strange, even perverse, to a Westerner, a life without sex! But we fail to remember that the sexual revolution of the 1960s is not that long ago. And in the meantime our society has been so sexualised with such easy access to pornography, that even children are now caught up in lust and are themselves lusted after.

No one needs sex. It's not like food. And since sexual desire is probably our greatest driver, can you imagine the relief when you are no longer hounded by sexual cravings as someone with OCD may feel when relieved of their compulsion.

Can you imagine the energy released for other purposes?

For the temporarily celibate, take the opportunity to find out how it feels when we let go of lustful thoughts. As with all acts of renunciation, we have to resist the fantasies, suffer the desire, feel it in the body, till the compulsive need exhausts itself completely to feel the release, the relief and the joy of liberation – even if only once!

And romance that blossoms often into an intimate relationship? This is also forsaken in celibacy. To someone seeking a greater love, such love is confining.

All the other loves – parent and child, friend with friend, even spiritual friendships– will all have a psychological dependency. This attachment is to be seen as unskilful, not evil. It has unwanted consequences. Such loves cannot be universal by definition.

True universal love arises when there are no particulars and can be arrived at only by relinquishing particulars.

The Buddha says our love should go out to the whole world, ourselves included, without any hatred or preference. In other words, whoever we meet within that given moment, whether we like them or not or whether they like us or not, they are the focus of our goodwill.

This will not be perfectly possible to do until the fences of the delusive sense of self are taken down. But we can begin the process of dismantling them.

When we are with someone, let us give them our full attention with the desire to know where they are coming from, how they feel, what they are saying. At the same time, let's be aware of the background of reactions and responses that arise within us. Let's develop an affectionate awareness and respond from the heart of goodwill.

In this way we can all in given moments, unhindered by erotic, romantic or specific loves, be celibate. This is the reason for celibacy – to develop unhindered love.

Difficult!

But worthwhile developing, because within the ambience of universal love, particular love finds a niche without that psychological dependency of attachment.

5
WHEN DOES LOVE BECOME CONTROL?

Along with the sense of self comes a desire to control, according to the Buddha. The self feels safe when it is has authority.

And why do we want this? Could it be that we have to gratify an unwholesome desire so that we feel happy? This strong desire is often called a need, though the term should really be applied to something essential – food and sleep on a physical level, for instance. Such unwholesome needs include anything we feel controls us– need for praise, success, sex, romance – even addiction to drugs and porn.

This need, now so essential for happiness, stems from a lack of self-love / self-acceptance, a deficit of inner worthiness, a want of dignity.

Such is its strength, it cannot see anything other than from the vantage point of 'me'. In other words, it very much becomes a definition who 'I' am. At the point where a 'take it or leave it' desire becomes a desire I need to fulfil, the other becomes the 'one' to fulfil that 'need'. If the other can't or won't do that, then the need to control arrives.

Many tactics are employed: Anger, withdrawal of services, silence, ignoring. Blackmail: 'If you don't... I will...' Petty spite or threats of revenge or self-harm / suicide, accusations of not really loving me. We'll do anything to bully the other into doing what we want them to do.

This way we can control children, friends, workmates, partners and spouses and all the rest of our relationships.

So paradoxically such unskilful needs that control us drive us to control others to fulfil them. And the more we feed them, the more demanding they become and the more we demand of others. It's a vicious circle.

It's not that we don't love the other. We show that when we treat the other as equal to us, not there to serve us, yet they may do so. Just as we are not there to serve them, yet we may do so.

We will know when our love is turning into control by our reactions whenever the other person refuses any of our requests. Can we hold still and wait for the unwholesome state to pass? Can we communicate with the other as other? If we can't at that moment, let's postpone it and talk later.

Let's find the time to contemplate and resist our unwholesome needs. At least then we feel we're taking back some control.

But often all we have to do is allow the need to manifest and hold it in kindness. Allow it to speak its feelings without words and wait for the turbulence to exhaust itself.

The heart knows how to comfort and heal itself.

SUNDRY REFLECTIONS

1
A NEW YEAR RESOLUTION

Resolution comes from the Latin 'resolvere' meaning literally to 'solve again'. That's what the new year offers us, an opportunity to reflect on the previous 12 months, indeed our lives, and consider how we can do better. One of the Buddha's constant exhortations is to reflect wisely.

We can and should consider our lives in many ways: The meaning of our work and leisure time; our relationships and our community; city life and nature; how we spend our wealth and our time.

Our reflections may be variously pragmatic, artistic, social and so on. But here we are concerned with the spiritual life – which we cannot split off from any other part of our lives. Instead we want to imbue everything we do with spiritual or ethical meaning. For it is the motivation behind our behaviour that manifests our wisdom or lack of it. Our objective, of course, remains liberation from all mental distress and awakening into a different relationship with ourselves and the world, free of strife.

What we do arises out of intentions which are present expressions of our attitudes. Attitude arises from our understanding. Reflection offers the opportunity to correct any misunderstanding that has arisen and in cases of uncertainty a spiritual confidant is helpful.

When we behave unskilfully and cause others to suffer, we create suffering for ourselves. The guilt and shame we may feel manifest a measure of compassion for if we neither loved or cared, we would not feel guilt or shame. So when these two mental states arise in our reflections, we know two things: That we have acted unskillfully; and that we have the compassion and love to do something about it. This leads to remorse which compels us to put right what we did wrong. Asking for forgiveness is a salve that facilitates reconciliation.

So does forgiving. Acknowledging the suffering of the one who has harmed us and the suffering we cause ourselves by holding grudges leads to the desire for reconciliation – no matter how painful that may be. And it is worth it because this is the pain of healing.

In the same way we need to develop that same attitude of forgiveness towards ourselves.

What ease there is in a heart free of guilt and shame! What ease when free of grudge and revenge! What ease when free of self-hatred and self-recrimination! Seeing the suffering caused by unwholesome thoughts, words and deeds, how easy it is to resolve to guard our thoughts, speech and actions.

But we must go further and that is to develop virtue. The Ten Perfections and the Four Illimitables offer us ways we can strengthen our character yet soften our hearts.

Finally, we reflect on the absolute necessity of our practice. We have been initiated and empowered into a practice, vipassana, leading to liberation. We reach a awareness that rises above the mundane and prevents us from entanglement and bewitchment. This in itself is a purification.

Here is one of the Buddha's best known aphorisms:

> Put an end to unwholesome behaviour.
> Do what is good for ourselves and others.
> Purify the heart.
> This is the teachings of all the Buddhas. Dhammapāda

The success of a good resolution lies in humility, to see ourselves as we really are. One resolution taken to heart and practised is better than a thousand we fail to accomplish. The path to hell is paved with good intentions. So we need to resolve what we know we can do. Start small. Do what we are sure is do-able. This leads to success and success breeds success.

Surely this coming year, our resolutions will bear great fruit.[6]

---

[6] New Year Reflections – https://www.satipanya.org.uk under Dhamma Talks/A Collection of Talks
Towards the End of Forgiveness: under Resources/Essays/All Essays

2

NEIGHBOURLY 'SOUNDS'

If you have never had to deal with a pounding bass line coming through the wall or the periodic flush or the muffled conversation of the TV or loud conversation – then you are lucky.

We may have ways of managing these situations. If not, the following might help.

First, become aware of the aversion and how it makes the ears glue themselves to the wall. Remember that this is the suffering, not the sounds. It is aversion that labels them as noise.

To cool our righteousness, recall times when we have been neighbourly nuisances.

Then – and this is the hard bit – always start with accepting the situation as it is: 'This is the way it is.' Keep repeating this gently in the heart until the heart lets go of: 'This is not the way it ought to be.' You may find the suffering disappears with the aversion.

Then ask: 'What can I do about the situation?' If there is something we can do, do it. If not, we just get on with the task in hand as best we can. As the aversion keeps snarling, repeat the exercise. It's surprising how the mind can blankout sounds once it has accepted them as normal audial background.

When I was a student, we rented a house right next to a rail line. The house shook with every passing. After a day or so, it never woke me up. But then the beer might have helped! Every time I returned to the East I had to get used to all the sounds. At Kanduboda it was the squirrels and other birds and wild animals. In Yangon, it was the traffic and the dogs. Two or three days later, I didn't 'hear' any of it.

But with the truly invasive, we can approach the neighbour knowing that if we are calm and equanimous we will always get a better result. Explain why the sounds are disturbing. Throw it gently back to them: 'I'm sure you wouldn't like it either if I played loud music.' Hopefully it works.

I had a neighbour who played Elvis – a lot. I was trying to prepare work for my classes. I gave up, mainly because I like Elvis and couldn't stop myself singing. I asked her to lower it a bit. She bellowed: 'I pay my rates.' 'So do I,' I answered, 'but it didn't include an Elvis disco.' After explaining and appealing to her better nature, she did as I asked. I was lucky.

If the situation becomes unbearable (and this does happen, especially if the sounds interrupt sleep), try getting in touch with the local authority since it has the powers to curb noise. Failing that, it is best to make a long-term strategy to move away, put it out there as an aspiration and work gently towards it.

May our neighbours be quiet, gentle and peace-loving!

3

SICKNESS

Sickness was a messenger of the gods, an awakening call that set Bodhisatta Siddharttha Gotama on the path to an astounding spiritual discovery.

When sickness befalls someone we know – a dangerous illness, a crippling accident – it comes as a jolt. It's happening around us all the time, but still we rarely strikes us. Now it's in our face.

When such misfortune happens to ourselves, it's a real shock. Depending on the circumstances, it may drive us to despair. A young policeman, all-body paralysed by a shot, chooses to commit suicide.

Even though illness is an everyday occurrence, we continue to live as if it won't happen to us. If we reminded ourselves every day of how vulnerable the body is, it would take away the tinsel armour of ignoring, of self-deception. Should I have to suffer, it won't be such a shock.

But a shock it will be, because so much of who we are, the Self, is tied up in the body. Sickness is a mini-death. It tears us away from what we love – 'the things I do; the friends I see; the job I have' – and offers us what we don't want –discomfort, pain, disability. The mind works on this and offers a future of horror, of terror.

Yet, here lies a gateway, an opportunity of escape, escape from the delusive world we have conjured up within ourselves and take for real. The escape cannot be yesterday, drowning in nostalgia. It's gone. Nor tomorrow, a world only in dreams. It hasn't arrived. The answer must be present. Right here. Right now.

That was the Buddha's astounding spiritual discovery. By developing right mindfulness, we can stand back within ourselves to discover an unassailable place. Even as the objective observer, the feeler, the experiencer, whenever it is stabilised, we've already found a haven. Indeed, when we have been patient enough to let all fear and aversion subside, this haven tells us there is physical discomfort or pain and disability to smaller or greater degree. And that's all!

There is no denying that is not an easy task. Indeed depending on the severity of the illness, it can be a great struggle. So let's start with the easy ones. Next time you are ill, even with a cold, try saying to yourself: 'There is this discomfort or pain and this illness prevents or hinders me from doing this. That's all.'

This sort of acceptance helps to establish patient forbearance that is uncomplaining and a realistic optimism that sees possibilities.

Here are some daily reflections to prevent us living in a make-believe world of continuous health:

> This body is subject to disease.
> This body is of a nature to fall ill.
> This body has not gone beyond sickness.

Such reflections act on the heart as toothpaste on teeth. If we want to free the heart of the accumulation of plaque from fear and anxiety, each day we need to face such possibilities. We get in touch with these unpleasant mental states and in accepting them, they manifest and evaporate. Far from making our lives gloomy, such reflections undermine the constraining effects of fear and anxiety and have the opposite effect of allowing our lives to bloom more.

Recognising the body's paramount importance in human existence and that this life form, as the Buddha tells us, is the best for liberation, we need then to turn our loving-kindness, metta, towards the body.

> May you be free of sickness and disease.
> May you be well and strong
> I determine to look after my body.
> Such blessings transform the energy of fear into care.[7]

---

[7] See Bodycare mp3: https://www.satipanya.org.uk under Dhamma Talks

4

LIVING IN THE NOW : PLANNING FOR THE FUTURE

So often we have to plan for the future. Marriages to organise, children's schooling to be sorted and always the shopping list and the shopping – and what will I do when I retire.

How can we live in the here and now, if we are forever planning a future?

Future planned events affect the present.

We wouldn't get up so early if it wasn't for the ungodly hour of the budget flight we've decided to take to Acapulco.

For this to have materialized the initial idea came to mind at a moment in the past. Perhaps it grew from a love of Mexican art – we really want to see Diego Rivera's murals. And we're interested in Mexican food. And there are miles of beaches and scuba-diving in a sea teeming with tropical fish, shipwrecks and even an underwater statue of the Virgin! The idea, laced with desire as such ideas usually are, evolved into a plan. Information was gathered. Decisions were made. The flight was booked. But we did not let desire confound us into a daydream. We have good purpose to go there – to appreciate the art, the food, the sea.

Let's take a different tack. Leafing through a magazine, we spot an advert for Acapulco. Everything dreamed of is there: Beautiful bodies on the beach soaking up the sun, glitzy nightlife, gorgeous restaurants, dancing till dawn.

The adventure, the food, the romance. Waking out of the reverie, the tea has gone cold. No matter, Acapulco it is.

The first planning was realistic and purposeful. The second, ungrounded, pie in the sky. The first should allow us to land with an open mind, exploring what has to be discovered; the second is mired in expectation. When we get there it rains, there's a nationwide strike, no one remotely attractive turns up. Can't wait to get away!

The first returns us home contented with the fruit of open-minded experience. The second dumps us home, disappointed, disconsolate with that awful feeling of having wasted hard-earned money.

The first planning was living in the now, planning for the future. The second was, while planning, living in a daydream and on arrival unable to live in the here and now!

5

MUSIC

Music is the language of the heart and can change our moods or deepen them, negatively and positively. No one doubts music's power over the heart, be it through pop songs, patriotic marches or symphonies. So it is as important to know what we put into our minds by way of adverts, reading matter, visual entertainment and so on, as it is what we put into our heart via sounds.

The sounds of nature from the song of a blackbird to the bark of a crow, the rustle of wind through grass to the clash of thunder, all resonate within the heart. And where there is emotion there is the body so that our emotional life also affects our physical well-being or lack of it.

In all monastic forms music plays an essential role. The chant offers the heart the ability to develop devotion. Even chanting Dependent Origination, more or less a list of physical and mental properties showing how suffering arises and ceases, becomes something more when we chant it. It is imbued with feeling, perhaps peacefulness or praise or thankfulness. This swells the heart with joy, welcome relief if it is otherwise weighed down with life's worries and cares. It is even more effective if we chant the Metta Sutta, the Discourse on Loving Kindness. And other auspicious chants are there to lighten the heart and fill it with quiet joy.

One way sound can be used to heal the heart of its negative states is this: Sit with a negative mood, say anxiety. Bury the attention into the feel of it, not allowing it to escape into the mind and create stories. (Remember it is through thought and imagination that the heart develops its unwholesome and wholesome attitudes.) Feeling an emotion or mood as simply a physical feeling allows us to see it for what it is – just a form of energy. Indeed, if we sink into it, we can describe its contents – agitation, nausea, heat, and so on.

Holding our position steady there, listen to some peaceful music – I suggest Allegri's Miserere Me (Oh Pity Me!) – see how the music creates another mood.

If classical music doesn't appeal, then any music that creates a sense of peace.

Maintain this mood in attention while not losing the sense of anxiety – and then sink that peaceful, loving mood into the agitation, the nausea, the heat.

This can never be a complete healing, of course, until the Three Roots of Acquisitiveness, Aversion and Delusion are eradicated. Indeed, until they are, unless mindful, we will continue to develop unwholesome states of mind.

But even so, music and the sounds of nature can be a balm to a burdened heart.[8]

---

[8] You may be interested in this website:
https://www.collegeofsoundhealing.co.uk/

6

TIME

Objectively, time is a way of measuring the distance between events: morning to evening, the passing days and years, between dental appointments, work and vacation.

But we don't experience time like this. It is often so slow. We wonder when it will ever end. Sometimes it's so fast we wonder where it's gone.

So how do we feel about time? How do we experience its passage? And how does our relationship with it make us use time?

Do we want to dominate it, be control? Are we frustrated when we don't get done what we ought to have got done in a certain time? Is there too little time to complete all those necessary tasks? Is time a perpetual rush? Are we crying out for more time?

Or is time fulfilling only when we are spending it with others? Time alone seems pointless, unsatisfying.

Or is time a bore unless something exciting is afoot? Living is more worthwhile the greater its emotional intensity.

Does time have to be useful? Must we always be doing something? Does doing nothing bring a hopelessness, even a despair? What's it all about if it's not about doing something, anything?

Do we feel we've all the time in the world? If it doesn't get done today, tomorrow will do. Why force this whole liberation thing? Meditate, meditate, meditate!!! Crazy. Relax. We're not going anywhere. There's nothing to achieve. Progress! For heaven's sake, let's just be happy with the way things are. Let us rest. Let us sleep.

I once watched a clock's second hand move round for two hours. I was pleasantly surprised that by the end of it, I felt calm and equanimous. I had done it to let go of the tyranny of 'do something'.

Now if time is a measure between events, our task is a way of being with events in a basically equanimous way.

Just as the ocean has a deep, steady flow and the surface is full of movement, so we need to find this deep steadiness and yet stay with the surface movement.

So in this context by time we mean living, we mean life as lived. But it also suggests awareness for without that we will be tossed hither and thither by the waves.

Time as flux: time standing still. To be still in the flux, that's the discovery – and the attainment.

Or to put it another way – go with the flow.

But then we must beware! As one wit pointed out – only dead fish go with the flow!

Christian mystics talk of nunc stans and nunc fluens – the still now and the flowing now.

7

TEA OR NIBBANA?

Whenever we take a break at home, at work or alone, how can we turn a cup of tea – herbal or proper, or coffee, with a biscuit – into a Dharma practice?

First, there is the intention and the intention always needs to be investigated. It may not be physical: The body does not need tea and definitely not coffee, nor is the biscuit necessary. In fact bread and water would do. Is it just greed, then?

How do we feel if we say – yes, it is greed? Sad? Sad at losing those delicious moments that brighten up the day. Sad, knowing at the same time that we simply can't renounce tea and biscuits and that this may very well be the great stumbling block on our way to Nibbana.

Let us remember that the Buddha did not teach self-mortification. He did not say that pleasure in itself was unwholesome, unless unethical of course. Taking pleasure in pinching someone else's biscuit and eating it is surely taking what is not freely given.

Now pleasure brings happiness. It affects our mental state. Happiness, born of pleasure that is not by way of indulgence, has in turn a good effect on the body.

So use this occasion to establish a wholesome state of mind. To do everything deliberately and with a sense of ease, we stop and make clear to ourselves our intention – to turn this tea break into a delightful ceremony.

Having chosen the beverage, stand sentinel at the kettle and wait for it to boil, continuing to let go of any agitation. Wait till the boiling has all but stopped.

Take time to make the drink. Stir the drink gently and quietly as an expression of our mental state.

Sit comfortably and gaze upon the tea and biscuit. Contemplate all the labour and expense involved – and the wonder of nature. We pay full attention to the process, to the tasting. We feel the bodily pleasure. We experience the mental state. Sip after sip, nibble upon nibble, we bring delight to the body, delight to the mind. Sip after sip, nibble upon nibble, we take the opportunity to share our joy with others. Family, friends, colleagues … all beings. May you be joyful! May your joy increase!

We sit with the empty cup and the plate, speckled with crumbs. How do we feel coming to the end?

Are we still aching for more, just one more biscuit? Is a subliminal desire now arising as unsatisfactoriness? Are we suffering the consequences of not acknowledging our indulgence? Does an existential angst arise at the thought that all good things come to an end?

Or is a quiet joy arising from an act well completed? Or are we sitting with a heart aglow with gratitude?

Or are we simply at ease, the body still, the heart calm, the mind silent and spacious? Are we ready for and open to the next moment? Let this be our aspiration: Oh, may my life end like this!

8

ON THE VIRTUE OF VISITING A CEMETERY

Visiting a graveyard is best done in spring – no better time to contemplate our mortality.

Every city, town, little village has cemeteries. They are ubiquitous. Wherever people live, there we will find graveyards. Because people die. In fact everyone who has lived has died.

Pretty obvious.

Yet even so we need to remind ourselves that life is short: 'Life is hard and then we die.'

At first this seems so negative. We love life. We want to live. Why talk about death, for heaven's sake. We all know death comes. We don't need to rub our noses in it.

In medieval times it was thought good practice to have a memento mori, an object in the house that was a reminder of death. The skull was thought to be especially apposite.

In Buddhist understanding too, death acts as a reminder of deeper truth. The Buddha said there were those who woke up even on the mention of death, others not till someone famous died, still others not until someone close died, and those unfortunates who didn't wake up till it was their turn to die.

Fat lot of use making sense of our lives on the point of death.

So there's a deep wisdom to be had in walking around the local cemetery. The same surnames crop up. Stones dating back two, three hundred years. Here they all are, our forebears. Their actions made our history.

Now at this very moment I am also making history and a time will come when it stops and this body will join them in a field or its ashes scattered into water or onto the wind – somewhere here on this earth.

'The way they came, I must also go. As their body is now, mine will also be.'

'Life is uncertain: death is certain.'

There's a certain comfort in knowing others have trod the same path. There's a relief in embracing a certain fate: 'This is the way it is.' But such reflections may bring a poignancy to our lives, may lead to resignation and eventually hopelessness.

Our path is imbued with a transcendent understanding, however. The Buddha taught that there was a sphere of experience with no birth and no death.

How can the contemplation of death and dying help us to experience Nibbana?

By contemplating death, we enter directly into the monster's jaws. Feel the terror and hold firm, knowing it is but a chimera. When the roaring ceases, we find it to have been but the delusion of a poor, sweating self.

9

A PET'S ENDGAME PRELIMINARY THOUGHTS

This essay came about because someone got in touch with me about their poorly cat whom they decided to attend to until she died.

Western understanding of animals begins with Aristotle who argued that animals had no moral responsibility and so no rights. But then slaves also had none – or women!

St Thomas Aquinas, the great Christian philosopher of the Middle Ages, declared animals had no souls, meaning that they were temporary creations by God who were annihilated on death because only souls were eternal.

The final nail in the coffin took away sentience from animals. Descartes said they were simply machines, automata – without reason or the capacity to feel pain.

The Buddha, on the other hand, as do India's other religions, declared animals sentient beings. Any pet owner intuits when their dog or cat is suffering just as we do when another human suffers. After all we only take their word for it. We cannot feel another's pain.

Again the Buddha taught that all sentient beings had tanha – unwholesome desire, but that all beings could act virtuously.

As we do, they took rebirth according to their ethical actions. This only makes sense if we define ethics in the broadest terms as relationship.[9]

So it seems we ought to treat dying animals as we would humans. We should take as much pain out of their dying process, make them as comfortable as we can and let nature take its course. If the pain cannot be relieved, then ending their lives may be the compassionate thing to do.

This brings into sharp relief what our personal intention might be to end a suffering animal's life. Is it because we ourselves can't bear to see them suffer? Or is it because it will cost too much to keep them going and they will die anyway. It may, of course, be too costly. Or have we not acknowledged that we don't want the bother of caring for an old or sick animal and therefore rationalise the killing?

Such motivations are unwholesome and will not improve our own karmic fruit. The one wholesome motivation would be compassion for our pet and the wish to relieve their suffering.

Supposing now we have various intentions in the mind – a familiar situation we find more often than not. When the time comes to decide, we ensure the right intention is the fully conscious one by repeating it to ourselves. This means we empower that intention and not the other ones.

---

[9] Do Animals Have Morals TED
https://www.ted.com/talks/frans_de_waal_moral_behavior_in_animals

10

MY BODY IS MOTHER EARTH

The abuse of nature did not really begin till the Industrial Revolution. But today's doctrine of consumerism has given it a quantum burst with its dominant dogma that the growth of possessions, whether things or pleasure giving services, equals purpose of life – now a globally held belief.

Ever since humans became self-conscious they created the 'other', be it the earth's minerals, its plants and animals. They have worked with nature to make life safer and happier, alas virtually always for themselves. The usual suspects – greed, aversion and fear – were soon manufacturing tools as weapons, grew food for warrior lords and trained animals for war.

This was true for the time of the Buddha.

Where minerals were once extracted by hard labour thus making them precious, giant machines now excavate in abundance and make them valueless. Where crops only grew by the sweat of the brow, giant machines till and harvest and make food cheap and undervalued. Where humans once lived close to animals, smelled their sweat, knew their pain and valued their work, giant machines have replaced them. Now, save for working dogs, we keep them as sentimental pets (few pet owners acknowledge the huge slaughter of other animals to feed them) and, of course, we eat some animals with disarming indifference.

How do we return to a relationship where we truly value minerals, plants and animals?

One way to contact nature is through our own very bodies. The Buddha asks us to contemplate the Four Elements. The Earth, its quality of weight, pressure. Fire, its qualities of heat, cold and temperature. Water, its qualities of cohesion and fluidity. Finally, air with its quality of movement.

Sitting, standing or walking especially outside, find these qualities in the body and nature. The hardness of bones and brick or stone; the warmth in our bodies, of the sun or the coolness of the wind; the elasticity of the chest breathing or a branch swinging; the feeling of movement as the body walks or the flight of birds. This is how we can experience the physical world, our earthiness.

The wisdom that grows from the realisation that we are in and of nature, leads to a heart connection – nature as Mother Earth.

We need only contemplate the minerals that make up the body, the food that keeps it alive, the air we breathe and the living beings, some that feed us, others that pollinate and those who make such glorious company – and all the microbes that live in our very bodies that manifest this symbiosis.

Our hearts need to absorb deeply how mothering earth, moment after moment, gives birth to this body and how this body is utterly dependent on mothering earth. We are but one breath away from death! Truly this body is Mother Earth.

I've tried to make myself more aware of this with a simple reminder coined from the verse on kamma:

'This body is born of Mother Earth, dependent on Mother Earth, fed by Mother Earth. However I treat Mother Earth, it will be to my own benefit or harm.'[10]

The Kamma Verse: I am my own kamma, I am heir to my kamma, I am born [in this life] from my kamma, I am the kinsman of my kamma, I am protected by my kamma. Whatever kamma I shall do, wholesome or unwholesome, I shall become their heir.

---

[10] The Kamma Verse: I am my own kamma, I am heir to my kamma, I am born [in this life] from my kamma, I am the kinsman of my kamma, I am protected by my kamma. Whatever kamma I shall do, wholesome or unwholesome, I shall become their heir.

11

THE ABSURD AND THE SUBLIME : A MIDSUMMER CONTEMPLATION

In the end there is an absurdity to it all. By absurdity, I mean a meaninglessness with a twinge of the ridiculous.

That life, consciousness and all we have experienced, have understood and come to love should come to end, makes for uselessness. Life as a pastime.

We can say: 'Well at least I enjoyed most of it. And I achieved this and that.' But that is to hide the absurdity beneath a pathetic self-indulgence and self-importance. To say 'my life is dedicated to the happiness of others' when we know their lives also lack the same meaning is a sorry attempt to make our lives meaningful.

Because of this, all human endeavour – science, politics, heroism, philanthropy – are all useless. And art too! So what point is there in trying to express anything when everything in itself has no intrinsic meaning? A piece of art is glued to its time and place, of interest to art lovers and art historians, but in the long run is veneer. Its focus is beauty and subjects personal, social, even cosmic, but rarely does it treat with the real problem. Which leaves us with the sheer absurdity of creating an object about a world and life that are inherently meaningless.

Yet paradoxically this is the game we must play. A game is a useless pastime. It need not be unwholesome in itself, but it is mere entertainment, save for the professionals, the fanatics and the financial managers who give to sport the meaning of their lives. How absurd is that!

When the Buddha-to-be realised at the end of youth what he was heading for, he suffered an existential crisis. He didn't want to leave his family and all he treasured but he had no choice. Capturing the full meaning of the Devadhuta – Messengers from the Gods (ultimate truth) – the sick, the ageing, the dead – he realised his destiny as a human being. He believed this would continue rebirth after rebirth and that simply added to the horror. The fourth Devadhuta was an ascetic sitting under a tree. This is what gave him an inkling of hope.

The horror of meaninglessness is what drives us to seek comfort in life's pleasures and joys and causes us to fight off and flee whatever turns us towards these dour Messengers.

By the time the Buddha sat beneath the Bodhi tree and made the Great Determination not to move until he had explored this meaninglessness or die, he had the invincible courage of someone who knows he has nothing to lose. If life was just a pastime after all, what would be left was to enjoy it as best one could. Such was and is the position of annihilistic scientific materialists. If it had meaning after all, then that would be the end of the despair of absurdity.

His realisation was an actual experience. He called it Nibbana. Although this word has been given various meanings, they revolve around non-attachment and liberation. Non-attachment was his new relationship to the world. Nothing mattered. Liberation was how he experienced this. 'Something' was set free. That something was intuitive awareness, Satipanya. Upon this realisation, everything mattered.

The Buddha realised that life's purpose was to bring this Satipanya to its own realisation. It was a rite of passage, a passage from ignorance and all the suffering towards Buddha realisation.

Asking why this should happen in the first place is deemed irrelevant: This is the way it is and this is the way we must go.

Again, all that seemed absurd now takes on profound meaning.

Our lives – personal relationships, work, even pastimes – take on the same meaning, journeying towards the same sublime destiny.

Art takes on the task of attempting to communicate the inexpressible. It will never succeed but try it must.

Seeing the delusive state of other people and knowing their potential, the Buddha had no choice but to teach. There he found meaning in his existence as a human being along with the flowering of his personal joy into the joy of helping others make their way to their own sublime destiny.

12

IF THERE IS NO SELF, WHO BEARS THE KARMA?

Every moment arises dependent on past and present conditions. This is no less true for the self, the sense of being a person.

Nowhere does the Buddha say – there is no self. While it is patently obvious to all that a self is there, he says it has no substance, lasting no more than a moment. There is only the process of I-making (ahamkara).

So a 'person', conscious and sentient, is arising and passing away all the time – even in sleep lies a sliver of consciousness and sentience or the alarm bell would not wake us.

The self or person is a collection of habits and the body with a consciousness of it all. Moments of self-consciousness arise where the person perceives they are a person.

Karma has become everyday speak for consequence, and within a person this manifests as the habits they have formed, both wholesome and unwholesome.

Now a person can only be in the present moment. Yet past editions of persons of today, all our yesterdays and even before that, have created acts of thought, words and deed – and all have continuing consequences.

If this person feels unhappy, it's to a greater or lesser extent due to the actions of a past person and this person now is bearing the consequences. And this person can act in ways that give rise to worse consequences for a future person. Similarly, should this person experience happiness because of right intention, this will determine happier persons in the future.

On the presumption that we will continue to arise as a momentary person for some time yet and possibly after death, if we want all future persons to be experienced to be happy, if only a moment each, we have to start doing and creating habits now that will make for future happiness.

This is loving oneself: When I'm happy, I really love being me!

Because a lot of this happiness depends on our outer circumstances, we have to try to steer that towards happiness. That means we engage with people and the environment in whatever way we can to enhance the happiness of ourselves and others. Depending on the situation, we'll want to express our involvement in joy, compassion, love, patience and so on.

This is loving the other.

So it is that an ethics born of the desire to make oneself happy is developed. And we can't do it without a self, without being a person.

Our task as human beings is to develop a continuous flow of happy selves. And help others do the same.

An added consequence is that it's so much easier to make spiritual progress when we are happy.

13

OVERWHELMED BY ALL THE VIOLENCE IN THE WORLD?

What can we do when we feel overwhelmed by the stories and videos coming from the seeming endless conflict between Israel and Palestine and the terrible images and slaughtering by Islamist fundamentalists – to mention two main areas of conflict?

To undermine overload, unrequited compassion, despair and burn-out try some of the following.

    a) It's a case of humility. Power: We need to accept what we can and cannot do and let go of trying to do something about a situation that we cannot fix. Consider this modern koan/paradox: What can we do when we've done everything we can do? Influence: We need to know what we can and cannot get other people to do and let go of trying to have influence where we have none.

    b) Take the long-term view. Look at Europe and its 1,000 years of internecine wars. That's how long it took, with events as horrible as those in the Middle East, until we finally agreed to live peacefully together. Of course, the carrot of peaceful co-existence and its benefits is there.

    c) we need to do what we can always do – send our goodwill messages of love and compassion. Even if we think it has no effect beyond ourselves it makes us feel we are doing what we can. In the Buddhist tradition, it is understood that goodwill and compassionate (metta/karuna) blessings will have an effect no matter how slight.

Donations can be made to the various relevant charities.

d) We need to know when enough is enough. Stop feeding the heart and mind with horror stories. Why stop at Israel/West Bank, Islamic State, Myanmar?

e) Finally, we accept that this is samsara where delusion will always play itself out, but also where it is possible for individuals to liberate themselves. This is the training ground.

14

LEGAL, MORAL, ETHICAL

We are often confused by what is legal as opposed to moral. It's legal to drink alcohol and smoke cigarettes, but is it moral? What the Buddha means by morality (sila) is those actions and speech that are skilful, wholesome and virtuous towards ourselves and others. Many laws plainly make unwholesome actions legal.

This is a consequence of our liberal society which takes 'religion' out of politics, preferring to leave moral questions of a more personal nature to the individual. If government interferes with our personal behaviour, it is accused of creating a nanny state – or worse, authoritarianism.

Unfortunately, making immoral behaviour legal takes the sting out of our immoral actions: 'Well, it's legal. So it can't be that that bad.'

The word ethical is fashionable these days. It is used to give the world of business and finance greater kudos. But while ethics has positive connotations, the word morality still carries Victorian undertones of guilt and shame.

The Buddha never fudged the question of which actions we should avoid – he gave us the Five Training Rules (sikkhāpada) – and he also encourages us to restrain the senses. This is balanced by the need to develop the qualities of friendship, compassion, reciprocal joy and so on.

If we accept ethics to mean the negative and positive aspects of our moral lives then we are accepting that our delusion or wisdom is expressed through our speech and deeds – and in our thoughts. So ethics is about how we relate to ourselves, others and the world. In other words, it is all about relationship.

Our ethical decisions are rarely a case of black and white, however, because we have to acknowledge situation and context.

One such dilemma arises with abortion. Once thought horrific and criminal, its legalisation softened the moral sting. In Buddhist understanding, consciousness arises at conception, no matter how dimly. The potential is there. So termination will always be a difficult ethical decision for those who see the foetus as a human being.

A similar dilemma arises concerning armed intervention. For pacifists, the taking of life is simply unconscionable, whereas others argue it can save lives.

A given decision is always rooted in intention and our responsibility is to make sure that our intentions, given context and situation, are for the benefit or the greater benefit of ourselves or others or both ourselves and others.

> Sikkhāpada: Training Rules(often translated as Precepts)
>
> To refrain from killing sentient beings
> To refrain from taking what is not freely given
> To refrain from abusing our senses (usually limited to sexuality,
> > but the word kama is sensual desire. That is not to indulge).
>
> To refrain from wrong speech –
> > lying, slander, coarse language and useless talking.
>
> To refrain from taking drinks or drugs that cloud the mind.

15

BARRIERS OR BOUNDARIES?

What is it about the self that creates such a mess? Could it be the hard lines it draws around things, people and events?

We go to a restaurant and we know what apple pie and custard should taste like. When we taste what we've ordered, we're disappointed. Of course, it might be that the pie is pretty bad. Years ago, my pie arrived and when I dug my fork in, the crust was so hard it broke into pieces that scattered everywhere. I wanted to ask the cook how much cement had gone into the pastry, but knew he wouldn't appreciate it. Looking back, if it had been my first experience of apple pie and custard, I might have thoroughly enjoyed it, knowing no different.

What about our politics? We draw hard lines around our views: 'I would never vote for …' Now we may not vote for that party. But what is the point of the hardness around it? It stops us acknowledging that there is some good in all parties. The undecided floating voter is considered weak and no political party likes them.

In relationships too we may have drawn comfort lines around our friendship group. Closed groups are cosy, but they are restrictive and self-serving.

This type of behaviour suggests a hardening, an inability to change even though change is all around us.

When our self-imposed barriers are being breached we feel threats arise to the status quo. Fear and aversion emerge. We react to protect, to maintain. Unless we can be mindful of our aversive reaction, a creative response is out of the question. We defend our positions, sometimes at great cost.

Boundaries are more fluid – the beach is sometimes the land and sometimes the sea. It's not that boundaries allow everything. They don't have to be porous. One can create conditions, but they allow us to be flexible.

When boundaries are being breached we experience an amorphous discomfort, a feeling of invasiveness, at worst a loss of personal dignity.

When I became a monk, I kept up my friendly easygoing relationship with people. This was fine, except when someone became familiar. Suddenly it was a slap on the back and 'how are you doing, Bodhi?' I felt at fault, trying to be a mate in a way that didn't accord with the dignity the Buddha demanded of his monastics. So that's when I asked people to address me as Bhante. It keeps a respectable distance between myself and the person I am talking to.

It also stopped me behaving sloppily, at least in public! I was lodging with a friend and I told him I was expecting a phone call at a certain time. Just beforehand, his phone rang. I reminded him that my call was due. Unfortunately, he heard this as a command. I got an earful which reminded me that hosts have their boundaries and I needed to respect these.

Should we be like the Cliffs of Dover or a beach that is sometimes the sea and sometimes the land?

16

UNWHOLESOME KARMIC RESULTS AS FATE

The psychological rule, as stated by Jung, says that when an inner condition is not made conscious, it manifests outwardly as fate. In other words, when the individual remains divided and is not conscious of his inner contradictions, the world must perforce act out the conflict and be torn into two opposite halves.

How true!

The Buddha talks of anusāya or latent tendencies lying underneath the obvious kilesa, defilements. Often, we are unaware of these subliminal attitudes and intentions.

One tell-tale sign that we are acting something out and are not totally or not at all aware of it is when we fall repeatedly into a similar unfortunate or painful situation.

Consider the do-gooder who consciously wishes in her heart to do only good for you, but doesn't realise she is controlling the situation, that she wants to help only because it makes her feel worthy and happy. Our ingratitude shocks her while all we feel is constrained, not-heard and even bullied. She doesn't understand why we gets so angry when all she is wants to do is help.

A retreatant of mine at Gaia House arrived with a set of garden tools and it was difficult for the co-ordinators to stop him doing what he wanted to the garden.

Consider the person who regularly falls in love and a few months down the line finds himself dumped! What's really happening is that, after the honeymoon period, he starts to criticise and be cruel, unaware that when the relationship becomes too close he finds it smothering. Yet he is madly in love. Not being conscious of the underlying attitude, he blames the other for oppressing him.

When we don't acknowledge that we feel insecure or angry or inferior we become sarcastic. Our sarcasm is funny to everyone but its victim. Making people laugh gives us back our self-worth, but mysteriously friends begin to avoid us.

If we look into our lives and see negative patterns, it may be time to have a hard look at our attitudes instead of blaming others or the situation.

In meditation, using the noting technique, if we remain sharp and perceptive we may catch these latent tendencies surfacing into our day-dreams.

This is how we can bring an end to the consequential fate of inner contradictions that Jung so clearly expressed.

17

IDEOLOGY LEADS TO STRIFE

The Buddha had this to say of opinions:

> A thicket of views, a wilderness of views, a contortion of views, a writhing of views, a fetter of views. MN 2. 8

When Master Kaccāna was asked by a Brahmin why ascetics fight ascetics, he answered:

> It is because of attachment to views, adherence to views, fixation on views, addiction to views, obsession with views, holding firmly to views that ascetics fight with ascetics. AN 2: iv,6 – Bhikkhu Bodhi: In the Buddha's Words

In this sense, a view is a tightly held belief, substantiated by personal experience and rational thinking with three components making it rock-like.

The first is the wrong view itself – diṭṭhi. Take the three predominant ones of the previous century: (i) The science of eugenics pointing to the purification of the race, a central tenet of Nazism; (ii) the revolution against capitalism and rise of the doctrine of the ownership of the means of production by the proletariat, giving rise to communism; (iii) the present politico-economy of neoliberalism, a free market driven by 'natural' forces, with its stress on privatisation, deregulation, fiscal austerity and free trade, without any social responsibility all leading to the recent and ongoing economic failures.

Added to this is the conceit – māna: 'I am right and everyone else is wrong.' In fact, they are so wrong they need to be annihilated or at least ignored. When the 'I' becomes a 'we', social upheaval is in the making.

And emotional attachment – tanha: One is prepared to give up one's life, sacrifice one's own spouse and children such is the devotion to the cause.

This is ideology and we see it in all religions, both conventional and secular. The previous examples were all secular, but the present day worst religious example of this is Islamic fundamentalism.

What is the escape from this continual strife?

First, the Buddha did not say we should not have views and beliefs. In fact, he had a clear view of what would help humanity: The Four Noble Truths.

Whatever views or opinions we hold, let them be held lightly as perspectives that can be changed and nuanced by others. We don't need to identify with them or own them, ours is just one view or opinion among many.

This demands humility which undermines conceit, for we may have misunderstood or only partially understood.

Although the Buddha pointed to a single right view on how to overcome suffering vis a vis the practical matter of living in the world, some have said he was a true pragmatist. Whatever works.

We can see this in how the rule (vinaya) for the Sangha was developed. It does not seem to have come from a preconceived ideal, but as time passed and the behaviour of monastics seemed inappropriate, rules were established.

One example concerns lay people who complained that monastics were coming at all times of the day on alms rounds and sometimes more than once! The Buddha established the rule that an alms round could only be done once in the morning and that all food had to be eaten by midday.

Another example is the celebrated change of mind concerning women joining the order. He had refused the request from women of his own family and court. Could women become liberated, asked Ananda, and if they could, should they not be given the same opportunity to join? The Buddha relented.

It's an interesting exercise to list all our views and opinions around religion, society, economy and politics. Then we need to ask: 'What makes me so sure I am right and the other is wrong? How do I react when someone disagrees with me? Have I really listened to the other with an open heart?'

If we find we have no strong views, ask: 'Do I need to put more energy into clarifying the beliefs that are guiding me through life? How might I do this?'

18

THE SACRED: ITS MEANING AND THE ROLE OF FREE SPEECH

The Sacred gives life its most profound meaning. It tells us why we are living – and why we must die. For myself, this is the Buddhadhamma, the teachings and practice as taught by the Buddha, and they provide my core values.

In Buddhism the Sacred is symbolised in the Wheel – originally a cart wheel. And the founder, teacher, exemplar and archetype is Siddhartha Gotama to whom we give the title, Buddha, the Awakened One. At first he was symbolised by a tree, an empty chair or footprints. But after 500 years, the Greeks –the first Westerners to be converted to Buddhadhamma – began producing statues.

The Sacred itself should not be confused with the way it is expressed through the speech and actions of human beings. For we are all deluded and our expressions are conditioned by history, culture and our personal experience.

Free speech and its companion free expression have never been absolutes. Avoiding discriminatory or prejudicial language protects minorities and any expression inciting violence is illegal.

Some say this freedom includes the right to insult, however. It is one thing to express our disagreement with another's views and actions with the intention to insult them. And another to follow the Buddha's own advice about right speech, that it should be kind, truthful and spoken / written at a suitable time. The purpose is to persuade the other to change their minds. So rather than coming from the heart of angry arrogance sparking only angry resistance in the other, the Buddha asks us to approach with humility – first understanding the other's position, then pointing out the errors and suggesting a different view.

The Prophet Mohammed is the founder, teacher, exemplar and archetype for over a billion Muslims. As in early Buddhism, his depiction in form is seen as a sacrilege, an offence against the Sacred. Whatever means cartoonists and political satirists have to lampoon, satirise and ridicule Islamists, turning the Prophet into a figure of fun does nothing but insult all Muslims. Not distinguishing the Sacred and its symbol from how it is used in this case has cost lives and it could even be argued that it is incitement to violence and therefore unlawful.

Buddhadhamma disavows all recourse to violence such is the commitment to harmlessness, though one is allowed to defend oneself. Even so the figure of the Buddha is often abused. In Afghanistan in 2001, the Taliban blew up the two great 6th century Bamiyan statues. At a more banal level is the use of the image for commercial reasons. For example, the Buddha in the lying posture advertises BA flights to the US that now offer beds. We also have a Buddha Bar and, of course, Buddha statues as pretty garden gnomes. And Buddha statues have even been used in pornography. One such case in Thailand scandalised the whole country.

Here Buddhists may feel constrained because to complain may seem an expression of attachment, to get angry a sign of weakness. But I see no problem in asking people to respect what others consider sacred. Respect after all is a facet of love. Only the most cynical materialists will fail to respond, paradoxically wanting their own views respected.

So this is a good moment to ask ourselves: 'What does "the sacred" mean to me? Do I hold anything sacred? How should I respond to someone who shows no respect for what I hold sacred?'

On a more personal note, I was in a new-agey knick-knack shop and a small statue of the Buddha was on the floor by the door. I told the assistant who I was and how offended Buddhists would be to see a Buddha statue where it could be kicked even inadvertently. I suggested placing it on a shelf – and when I went in next time it had been moved.

We bought toilet cleaning material with the Buddha image on it and I phoned Tesco. The assistant said she would contact the manufacturers.

Even if the statue was sold and the Tesco assistant raised her eyebrows and simply did nothing, slowly but surely the message might get across that some things need to be respected. [11]

---

[11] You may find Free Speech: A Very Short Introduction (Very Short Introductions) by Nigel Warburton as useful as I did on this topic.

19

AIM AND OBJECTIVE IN TIME PRESENT

Our concept of time is linear in that we believe we are coming from a past, we stop for a moment in the present and then head off into the future. Historically speaking this is true. We can point to past happenings and to some extent predict future happenings.

These views can be considered conventional. From a personal viewpoint, time is how we structure events. If I said to you, I went for a walk yesterday afternoon, you could position that walk in, not today, not tomorrow. All this is useful for daily living, but can be a barrier to experiencing time in a liberated way.

How can we liberate ourselves from time? First, acknowledge that it does not exist but is a concept whereby we organise past, present and future events. We don't want to get rid of the concept – if we did, we'd be utterly disoriented. But we need to recognise the disconnection with present events that may come with it.

This moment is sandwiched between what we think has happened (memories are never absolutely accurate) and what we presume will happen. So we are either compelled to act in a certain way determined by a past decision or are acting in a way dictated by a future we imagine or expect. So we are never living in the present moment as it is right now.

When we behave like this, we're not in contact with how things really are. In fact, we often find ourselves in conflict with what is actually happening or we're manipulating what is happening to realise a future event. We live neither in the future nor do we experience the present moment as it is.

One way we can bring ourselves into present time is to make a distinction between aim and objective. Suppose we have to go to the dentist (I prefer uplifting examples).We set off and the aim is to get to the dentist on time. The objective is to stay mindful of what is happening every moment of the way. This may include any anxiety about being late or thoughts about what may happen.

This way we're always living in the present even though we may be experiencing the consequences of past action, the toothache, and the effects of future action, the appointment.

In other words, it is to live in the immediacy of the present moment.

We catch ourselves opening a door: Are we already in the other room? Catch ourselves brushing our teeth. Are we in a hurry to get it over with, so we can leap into bed? How often have we set out and reached our destination without any awareness of the journey? How many times have we 'mislaid' our keys?

Realising the frequency of missed present moments will make us want to do something about it.

20

IN WHAT WAY SHOULD BUDDHADHAMMA AFFECT OUR POLITICS?

A Moral Politics

Given that government, in theory at least, is our common will, representing us as a people, how do we define ourselves? Will we come to the aid of those among us struggling to get by or will we throw the needy back upon their own meager resources? Is the prevailing philosophy of governance one of mutual concern and collective help, or one of stark individualism in which everyone has to fend for themselves, or at best rely on charity? This is not so much a political question as a moral one, a question pertaining to the moral basis of our common life. Much depends on how we answer it. Bhikkhu Bodhi, A Moral Politics

In 2016, the referendum on Brexit and Donald Trump's election in the US conveyed one stark reality about democracy: Most of us, myself included, don't know enough to make a truly informed vote. And the 'information' given by parties, newspapers, social media and other data outlets is generally skewed towards their own bias. Indeed, all of us vote from a biased angle – our preference.

Politics is about power. So when we vote, we put someone in power over us. When a person or party has that power, they can change our society, our national and local communities. When an election comes around, this is the only time that we, ordinary citizens, have a chance to affect the political landscape and, by extension, the society we live in.

The Buddha got involved in the politics of his time, directly and indirectly. Though a very different society, the moral problems around power were similar.

When a dispute arose over the water rights of the Rohini River between the Buddha's own clan, the Sakya, and the neighbouring Koliya clan, he went to pacify a situation that threatened to turn into a war. He asked them what was more precious, the water that ran in the river or the blood that ran in their veins?

The new young king of Magadha, Ajātasattu (who starved his father to death), sent advisers to ask the Buddha if it was a good time to attack the Vajji Sangha, a democratic republic. The Buddha enumerated the qualities that made a sustainable sangha, the monastic order. The king took this to mean it was not the right time to attack. But by subterfuge he worked to undermine those very qualities the Buddha had obliquely praised and so he eventually conquered them.

Whether the Buddha would have voted or not, is moot. But for us today, there is party politics and real people issues out there to be considered – and voted on.

In our times community issues abound – immigration, NHS, armed intervention, the financial sector, EU, climate change and so much more. How can we guide ourselves through all this rather than box ourselves in by our own views, opinions and, worse, by our unacknowledged biases? How can we avoid being swayed by popular demand?

The term political correctness once described a means to avoid prejudice and discrimination in our language. Nowadays, it is a pejorative term, used to stifle debate and criticism and to denigrate those who object to a consensus.

It is instructive to make a list and write out what we want to happen in our society and why. Then question those assumptions by considering what those opposed to our positions are saying, to be open to their arguments. We listen and are not afraid of being hoodwinked or brainwashed or converted. It may surprise us that opposing arguments also have strengths. We may move to a more nuanced position.[12]

---

[12] Talk on TED by Jonathan Haidt. Although the talk is about US, the general orientation of conservative v. liberal/socialist is universal
http://www.ted.com/talks/jonathan_haidt_on_the_moral_mind?language=en
Transcript: The moral roots of liberals and conservatives
Is this why liberals (small l) become conservative (small c) in later life?

21

PRACTICE MAKES PERFECT[13]

Practice is repetition. Think of the footballer, the piano player, the actor. Even if we want to become proficient on the keyboard, we have to practise. I myself have become fairly proficient in the two-finger chopsticks technique!

Now we can't practise for the sake of practice. Repetition would be meaningless – a hell realm, even – if the aim was simply to repeat and repeat. Consider Sisyphus, the King of Corinth, whose trickery and deceit earned him eternal punishment from Zeus. He was forced to roll a huge rock up a hill in Hades and every time he reached the top, it rolled back down towards him for ever and ever. That's tough!

Practice requires an aim and it's this that should give us the courage and tenacity to keep going with it. Again bring to mind the dedication of Olympic athletes.

So we should endeavour to be spiritual athletes. Luckily this needs no physical prowess or intellectual brilliance – in fact we don't need any special talent at all. What we need is confidence in the vision that we are capable of perfect contentment and happiness.

---

[13] This phrase is used by a man who is a legend in American football coaching, Vince Lombardi. He actually said: 'Practice does not make perfect. Only perfect practice makes perfect.'

To achieve this, the Buddha has given us a technique, vipassana, and instructions in how to maintain right mindfulness in ordinary daily life. Everything boils down to this right awareness.

And when he talks of living the life guided by the Dhamma, it is always based on the virtues – the emphasis being on Metta, that universal quality of good will to all beings.

In our sitting practice, the repetition starts with settling on the breath. And then we repeatedly bring ourselves back to the presenting event, what's actually happening now. That's the practice. Insights arise naturally into the three spiritual gateways of awakening:

- a) Understanding how we create suffering
- b) Experiencing the reality of impermanence
- c) Realising the false identities and possessions we are creating

Insights are rarely shattering experiences, but moments of recognition, acknowledgement, mostly reinforcing and deepening what we have already seen.

In ordinary daily life, this mindfulness is conjoined with ethical behaviour and the very life we lead is the practice. Much of our daily life is repetitious: The morning ablutions, the eating, the job. And yet each event is naturally a little different from the rest. Even so the practice is bringing this-moment-attentiveness to bear with a good heart.

With an aim, all repetition becomes meaningful but that doesn't translate into dedication. That comes by exercising the virtues, raising enthusiasm and resolve, a real heartfelt commitment. Resolute practice underpins awakening.

If all we have is the aim, some vision as to the future attainment, and no practice, then the spiritual life enters the world of fantasy and disappointment.

The Buddha did not become Buddha by aspiration alone.

22

SCIENTISM MEETS BUDDHISM (BUDDHADHAMMA)

Some of us have feet firmly cemented in the empirical objective truths of science, with hearts dedicated to the Buddha's teachings and heads that negotiate an understanding between the two that gives direction to our lives.

Unfortunately coming to the Buddha's teaching from a belief that the scientific method of observation, hypothesis and repeatable experimentation is the only way truth can be determined means some of his ideas must be discredited as unprovable, with added subtext that it is all deluded imagination. Such is 'scientism'.[14]

The teachings can also be 'proved' false by approaching them from a particular viewpoint (hermeneutics). Because the Discourses are not the Buddha's exact words, only a minute portion might be verbatim, so additions and interpretations probably abound. This allows us to form our own interpretation.

So we might decide that concepts such as rebirth were introduced to align Buddhadhamma with prevailing ideas of reincarnation to make the Buddhadhamma more palatable. Presuming the Buddha did not teach rebirth

---

[14] Bertrand Russell: Religion and Science p 242: Whatever knowledge is attainable, must be attained by scientific methods; and what science cannot discover, mankind cannot know.

or any form of afterlife puts him in the annihilationist camp. And this means Nibbana can be only: (i) momentary, (ii) or if attainable as a constant state by an occasional person, comes to an end at death. It cannot be a transcendent state beyond space and time, mind and matter,

A cultural bias of ours is that only the scientific method can determine what is true. This extreme view denies that for every individual an inner, personal, private, non-repeatable experience is an event as real as an eclipse of the moon.

The Buddha did not conduct objective experiments to prove his teachings. So there is no instance of control groups where one set is given the Four Noble Truths with the practice of vipassana, another a set of Ignoble Truths and vipassana, and a third, no truths at all with vipassana to determine the quickest way to awakening.

The Buddha's phenomenological approach is about our personal experience of life. When he talks about the world, he sometimes calls it the All. He is referring not to the objective worlds out there that science investigates, but how we sense, feel and react to the inner world that appears in consciousness – the world out there as perceived by the individual, plus all the sensations, emotions and thoughts. The two approaches can be very different. Take time. Scientifically we can measure a minute but as a personal experience a minute can flash by as we watch a film or crawl along as we wait for the kettle to boil.

Out-of-body experiences or a past life recall are as true as gravity for those who experience them and are often life changing. Nibbana by definition is unprovable to the sciences. The Buddha tells us that experience contains nothing of the material or mental worlds and yet insists it is never changing and the greatest happiness of all.

For those of us not entirely convinced of Scientism (the secular belief that only matter exists and everything is 'an emergent property' from it) but who can't trust the concepts of rebirth and a transcendent Nibbana, the optimum position to take is perhaps 'don't know' or 'not sure'. Coming to a conclusion is not compulsory, for so long as honest doubt guides our investigation, we will come to know for ourselves through our own direct experience.

If you don't know, hang loose. You never know!

Here are two books, downloadable and donation only that collect a lot of the sayings from the Discourses around Nibbana and the process of awakening and a book that tackles rebirth. Don't be put off by the title. It is quite readable.

            Mind like Fire Unbound by Thanissaro Bhikkhu

The Island by Ajahns Passano and Amaro

Rebirth and the Stream of Life: A Philosophical Study of Reincarnation by Mikel Burley

23

OUR BASIC DISPOSITION TO LIFE

Just as most cafes these days have background music (and often not so background), so our psyches have a background tune(s). Getting to know our own basic disposition is enlightening.

The ways to categorise characters and personalities according to a fundamental nature are legion.

From ancient to modern times, the dominant categorisation was the notion of the Four Humours or Temperaments, connected to season, age, organ – used also to diagnose the cause of illnesses

The four fundamental personality types were:

> Sanguine: Enthusiastic, active and social, optimistic and over-enthusiastic.
> Choleric: Independent, decisive, goal-oriented, but also aversive and reactive.
> Melancholic: Analytical, detail-oriented, deep thinker and feeler, but also sad, shy.
> Phlegmatic: Relaxed, peaceful, quiet, but also lethargic and unconcerned.

(Wikipedia)[15]

---

[15] Amita Scmidt Buddhist Personality Types:

We pass through such states multiple times during a day, but usually one underpins all as a motif – an attitude we have developed towards life.

Other typologies include the Myers-Briggs. One worth exploring if you haven't already is the Enneagram [16] – a great and very helpful discovery for me.

Only in later Buddhist commentaries were such personality types developed. You will not be surprised at their categorisation. Yes, you've guessed! The greedy, the aversive and the deluded character. Their opposites might seem a little strange: Faithful, discerning and speculative (not the opposite as we shall see). With Dhamma practice, the one moves towards the other.[17]

Greed seeks to gratify itself, whereas faith, better translated as confidence, also desires to get, to achieve, but what is virtuous. We would normally think of generosity as the opposite, but here we see how close greed and confidence are.

Aversion holds objects at a distance but condemns them, whereas discernment also sees objectively, but is judicious. Again we would normally see the opposite as love, but here again we see how anger distorts our perception.

Delusion is a state of confusion whereas speculation thinks itself undeluded, but gets lost in all sorts of 'thinking'. It seems the Commentaries give no hope to the deluded! But obviously as delusion is undermined, wisdom arises. So since we are all, save the arahants, deluded to some extent or another, we need to question our thinking. But we can still live in hope of illumination.

We can tell which type we are if we catch how we think and how we do things.

If we detect a fundamental disposition, it is good to ask: Is it wise? Is it beneficial? If not, then we need to counteract it.

---

https://amitaschmidt.com/wp-content/uploads/2017/11/personality-types.pdf

[16] There is even an Institute – https://www.enneagraminstitute.com/
[17] For a more detailed exposition of the Personality Types in Early Buddhism: Buddhist Character Analysis Robert Mann & Rose Youd https://www.aukana.org.uk/
For those of you, who have a copy of the Visuddhimagga by Buddhaghosa, you will find the Temperaments on Page 102 para 7
https://www.accesstoinsight.org/lib/authors/nanamoli/PathofPurification2011.pdf

For instance, if a basic attitude is an amorphous feeling of guilt (aversive / melancholic), then we undermine this by remembering our unethical actions. Either apologise for them or make amends. If that's not possible, then accept whatever consequences may arise. Don't obsess over it! Instead, we bring to mind all our virtuous actions and congratulate ourselves.

If it is beneficial, be mindful that there is often an overplay. An optimistic joy (greedy / sanguine) can lead to over-expectation and disappointment. Experiencing disappointment is a warning signal to us to make reality checks.

24

THE WISDOM OF UNCERTAINTY

Idappaccayatā is a long Pali word translating as the Law of This and That or Specific Conditionality. In this very simple verse lies the understanding of why we live in an uncertain world:

When this is, that is.
From the arising of this comes the arising of that.
When this isn't, that isn't.
From the cessation of this comes the cessation of that.

Two lines of events converge on the ever-present moment that is the event we experience all the time – just this moment. Are we talking about inner conditioning meeting external circumstances?

All events originate in the past – a linear cause and effect process. We can cause them or something else can. If we play the lottery every week, we have just that less to spend– a direct cause by an action we made. But one week we win a shed-load of money. That is because a computer picked the winning numbers we selected, not because we bought a ticket. To think we might deserve the money is superstition. And if we resisted the temptation to play the lottery none of this would happen!

In each moment, however, various lines of past events converge and this is true of every moment of our lives.

A newspaper reported that a man who was drunk stepped outside the pub to take a breath of fresh air and managed to fall down a bank that bordered a road. That very moment a car was passing the spot. Two lines of past actions collided and the poor man was killed. That he ended up rolling down a bank and landing in the middle of the road is his own doing, but the collision was caused because someone else decided to drive along that road at that time. To think the events are connected save by happenstance or to think he deserved to be killed is superstition.

If he hadn't got drunk, none of this would have happened!

Two contemplations arise out of this understanding. The first is that we don't know the consequences of our actions. Doing something wholesome doesn't guarantee a beneficial outcome. Since we don't know the matrix into which we are making an input, we could very well be doing the wrong thing.

The second is that the inward effect is beneficial. Our inner moral life grows with every virtuous action. And again because we don't know the matrix of our own heartmind, talking a homeless person, making contact in a way we haven't before with homelessness, may lead us to join a charity or even set up a charity.

Nor do we know what will happen because someone else has made decisions or because nature produces its own events.

A lot of our time is fairly predictable. We live in a reasonably ordered society. Events that contradict our expectations are seldom enough to cause us surprise or shock. In a war zone, that wouldn't be the case. But our feeling of security can easily be shattered, for example by a sudden death.

If every morning we spend a moment contemplating the day's unknowability, we will fortify ourselves against shock. Nor will be we become overexcited by surprises.

By not being bound by 'what will happen', such contemplations open the day to possibilities. It undermines anxiety and makes us more flexible. We can adapt more easily to unforeseeable events. Herein lies a lesson from uncertainty.

25

WHY ARE WE ASKED TO OBSERVE ANICCA – IMPERMANENCE?

As we become aware of how everything we experience is a flow of events, comings and goings, this understanding slowly percolates through the system and changes our relationship to beings and things. As the Buddha says: 'Nothing in the world is worth holding on to.' Why? Because nothing remains anyway.

Clearly perceiving impermanence undermines dukkha – suffering and the unsatisfactoriness of attachment.

In Mahasi vipassana we are asked to observe more minutely, however, which is why we make the great effort to slow down. Slowing down the body slows the mind. Stopping and noting intention returns us to an awareness of momentary moments.

As this focus intensifies, time fragments into minute moments of arising and passing away. We are not seeing the world out there arising and passing away, but individual acts of cognition. The amazing thing is that when a moment of cognition comes to an end, still there is awareness.

This is how we come to realise that we are not acts of cognition, which include all the khanda, the Aggregates. Our physicality, perceptions, feelings, mental states and acts of cognition are not me, not mine, not a substantial self.

Thus perceiving impermanence helps us to realise anatta – Not-self.

The corollary is to experience what we are – that awareness. Awareness is the deathless.

This is a momentary dropping of the fetters of ignorance and delusive desire. A moment, like a flash of lightning into Nibbana.

So by observing impermanence we comprehend both suffering/unsatisfactoriness and anatta not-self. But more, we come to realise that awareness, sati, is itself the One Who Knows – Buddho!

Bringing this observation of impermanence into ordinary daily life is simple – whatever we're doing, when it finishes, STOP! Acknowledge that that action of thought, speech or deed has come to an end and will never happen again.

It may be that the emotional attachments begin to rise there and then – nostalgia, grief, disappointment and so on. If we can wait for these to pass, all well and good. Otherwise recall the incident at the evening meditation and let them burn out there.

In this way, in ordinary daily life, we become aware of impermanence, of how attachment causes suffering. In allowing it all to rise and pass away, we realise that none of it constitutes a permanent self or me. Nothing can actually be possessed. It is all not me, not mine.

26

DEALING WITH INTENSE EMOTIONS AND MOODS IN ORDINARY DAILY LIFE

Let's focus on how we create more misery out of misery.

Often in daily life we have to deal with intense and painful emotions. They may be short or can carry on for days, even years.

I once walked across a bus station and the station master set upon me. In no mood for a fight I meekly listened to his criticisms. He went on about how drivers wept when they backed into people and injured them. I had thought we were talking privately, but when I turned to go, quite a queue had formed in the shelter and people overheard our one-way conversation. The look of breathless pity an elderly woman gave me said it all. Well, that shame hung around for years!!! And so did the imagined replays of my indignant retorts. What the French call l'esprit d'escalier – staircase wit or riposte.

There are moods too, those longer lasting emotional states that seem to run subterranean and surface every so often like horror ghouls – the usual culprits of depressive, anxious and aversive moods.

We must first remind ourselves to stop the mind restarting its story. We can be sure it's again cranking up the emotion and empowering it a little more. This is the path to despair, to suicide or murder. If we catch ourselves lost in the same old narrative, we must surface from it at once, sink into the body and stay with the feeling.

But when there's no time to do that or the stories are persistent, we need a break from it all. That's when we tend to fall into the error of suppression. We let aversion or fear push it out of our minds and we seek distraction. But the more we push it away, the more energy we unwittingly give it for now it also has the force of our aversion. It's like pushing a spring down. When we let go, it jumps back with more force than when it first uncoiled because of the extra force it has had to absorb.

But we can learn to park an emotion or mood. We can talk to it and say: 'I will attend to you later, but now I need/would like to attend to this.' Notice the word 'attend' meaning to pay attention to, to wait upon. Gently put it to one side and turn the attention elsewhere.

Even if it's lurking in the background, we can occasionally turn a gentle smile towards it and assure it that we will attend in time.

Then, of course, the time to attend must be found!

27

HOW MUCH PAIN, PHYSICAL OR MENTAL SHOULD WE SUFFER?

How much pain and suffering should we bear? This question needs to be referred back to primary aims – the one to purify and strengthen the heart, the other to end delusion through insight.

If the pain and suffering are bearable, they become a vehicle to develop patience, equanimity, affectionate awareness and insight. Once we feel, if only temporarily, that we have reached that limit, then it seems wise to find a way to wind up or assuage the pain.

For instance, in sitting meditation aching knees are well documented. Unfortunately, the knees don't bend that way and relief comes only when the tendons at the top of the legs lengthen. In the meantime, we have to deal with the pain. So long as it's bearable, we can continue to investigate, and when all the effort goes into enduring pain, at least we are developing forbearance. A point may come when it's just too much and it seems wise to change posture rather than grit the teeth, clench the jaw and be praised for an heroic stance against pain. Our unshakeable endurance! We may find we have damaged our knees. This has happened. In fact, I began to have a loose cartilage myself at one point in early Zen practice.

But when circumstances completely undermine the process of spiritual investigation, what point is there in suffering them – save, of course, to build up that quality of endurance. Even here we have to be careful.

A meditator once told me he had a very bad toothache. I asked why he did not take an aspirin until he could see a dentist. He said he was building up the virtues needed for greater suffering. 'Suppose there will be no greater suffering for you?' I asked him.

It seems to me we should match endurance with the quality of investigation. To do otherwise may indeed be an act of pride: 'I'm bigger than pain.' Such an attitude leads us into self-mortification which the Buddha found to be meaningless torture. Endurance should be balanced with care of the body.

For those in dreadful pain, the option of suicide, always a delicate topic, may arise. What is considered bearable or unbearable is subjective, always personal and individual. It's generally understood that only fully liberated beings can take their own lives without unwholesome karmic consequences. But this has been questioned.

It is important to remind ourselves, however, that understanding how suffering and unsatisfactoriness (dukkha) arise, we need to know that the given, be it physical or mental pain and all illnesses, may have a multitude of causes. But in contrast our relationship to them (aversion, fear, despair) is self-generated. To investigate how we create suffering and unsatisfactoriness is a path to liberation via understanding the Second Noble Truth – the cause of suffering is unwholesome desire, tanha.

28

TO BECOME OR NOT TO BECOME

The Buddha lists three types of wrong desire or taṇhā.

Kamataṇhā covers all our day-to-day desires. Bhāvataṇhā is the desire to become, where the self wants to recreate itself time after time. Vibhāvataṇhā is the desire not to become, which is not as well publicised as the previous two.

We're familiar with our everyday desires to do something, to enjoy life and get away from what upsets us. We are all aware of wanting to continue to live – well, maybe not all the time. Occasionally, we want to escape ourselves so we slump into the armchair and fall asleep. When things get really bad, we may even want to stop living altogether and wish we were never born. So we all experience these three desires now and again.

But the desire to continue or not to continue refers to a deeper positioning, manifesting in belief systems that presume the 'I' endures or does not. The Buddha called such systems eternalism and annihilationism. His teaching did not sit in either category because these beliefs were based on the notion of a self.

Annihilationism, often confused with materialism or nihilism, is used in Buddhism as opposite term to eternalism. It is the belief that when a person dies, that's it. All beings live only once.

Materialism, especially scientific materialism, believes everything is an emergent property arising out of matter. So thoughts, emotions and consciousness arise primarily out of the material of the brain and nervous system.

According to the OED, nihilism 'rejects all religious and moral principles, often in the belief that life is meaningless'.

Annihilationism, unlike materialism, can also include a finer energy, mind, as well as matter but that too will annihilate upon death. Unlike nihilism, it does not necessarily reject religious and moral principles, there's just no belief in an afterlife.

When we sit deep within ourselves, we may touch upon our deepest intuition about life and death. Perhaps we feel life is worthwhile and has a meaning beyond itself, that is 'I' am worthwhile, 'I' am meaningful and 'I' will continue to live after death. Or we may intuit that life is not worthwhile and has no meaning beyond itself, that is 'I' am ultimately insignificant, 'I' have no intrinsic value and 'I' will not continue to live after death.

Just because I believe I am eternal doesn't mean life is all roses. Just because I think life is ultimately meaningless, doesn't mean I'm not going to have a good time or behave ethically.

So long as there is a self, we will veer to one or the other of these opposites and this will be reflected in our understanding of the Buddhadhamma. Eternalists tend to think of Nibbana as an eternal state of Buddhahood that 'I' will enjoy – 'someone' who is a Buddha. Annihilationists will deny that the Buddha ever taught there was a transcendent and if there is, it is only momentary.

The answer lies in the careful investigation of that very sense of self, the feeling of being 'me', whenever such a sense or feeling arises. We can also reflect when it has not been there – even in ordinary daily life.

The Buddha says Nibbana was not created nor does it die. So it must be here. He says it doesn't arise and pass away which is another way of saying the same thing. So it must be constant.

So what could 'it' be?

29

FAIRNESS AND EQUALITY

Children often have an acute sense of fairness: 'It's not fair!' They feel they've been treated unjustly and indignation, anger, often tears follow. This we take into adulthood. But what do we mean by fairness in a world manifestly differentiated?

We talk about equal opportunity and that presumes we are all at the same starting line. In the 100m dash, it would not be fair if the starting blocks were unevenly spaced or if in the 1,500m race the curves were discounted. But levelling the playing field is not how real life works and it is certainly not how it all begins.

Consider our educational system, banking system, celebrity system pay scales, indeed consider those of the now 'chief executives' of charities – the whole capitalist system.

That's when doubt alerts us to the understanding that fairness and equality are interlinked. And this morphs into the notion that we should all have the same, even though we are not the same.

The Western concept of equality emerged with the idea of an all-powerful, but ethical God. Although he made everyone different, that is not equal, in his justice system we are all equal. This is enshrined in our law – we take into consideration mitigating circumstances. After all, that's only fair.

There is something about fairness that strikes true since it is such an enduring concept.

In the Buddha's teaching on why things happen lies the concept of unknowability and uncontrollability. Things happen due to past causes and in the very present that we can neither foresee or influence. Life is a series of happenings, of events over which we do not have total control, or only minimal control or sometimes no control at all. We might win a jackpot or get hit by a kipper – out of nowhere.

The Buddha does, however, point to a fundamental justice, a fairness, an ethical law – the law of kamma. When we think, speak or act with harmful intent, we do harm to ourselves and others – with consequences. And vice versa – goodness will produce goodness. This law applies equally to all.

But this tells us nothing of how consequences unfold. For whenever we think, speak or act, we send a force into a matrix of relationships, out into the world and into our interior world. Eventually, though not at first apparent, our virtuous empowered intentions begin to manifest in better inner and outer worlds. But our final goal is a happiness independent of either inner or outer worlds, Nibbana. And that is equally available to us all.

Fair enough! But it does mean we have to tread carefully, wide awake and ready to take spiritual advantage of the unexpected, both fortunate and unfortunate.

30

SILENCE

Our world, the culture we live in, is drenched in noise. The sounds of traffic, machinery, the music that makes it hard to hear and speak in cafes. Even in the train's Quiet Coach someone has to speak so everyone else can hear.

On the streets, in the offices and parks, people walk with their smartphones, forever communicating, listening, looking. Deaths on the roads are caused by smartphone enchantment.

Every sense has its mode of rest. Smelling and tasting are the more sensitive the less they are put to work. Sight is rested easily with closed eyes. Touch softens in rest. But even in sleep, the ears are awake. How amusing it is to see a sleeping dog's ear prick on a sound. And the mind chatters incessantly, silenced only in deep sleep.

Sounds are neutral, but some we experience as music and others as dissonance. Music, whether human or of nature, is nurturing – but it too can need stilling. Noise creates tension and if constant can cause ill-health. There comes a craving for the end of sound, the succulent pleasure of silence.

But the mind? It won't stop so easily. In the quietest of meditation rooms, it blasts out. Not just chatter, but emotional disharmony too. All the aversions, anxieties and lusts.

Shutting down the outer world with its music and noise only opens up the inner world – for most –of purgatorial videos. We can draw the concentration down to the breath's neutral sensations and listen to it, feel it, let it coax us into stillness and the delightful joy of silence.

For those with ability and time, there is a state of absorption of sheer stillness, peace and absolute silence. But even to sit quietly with a cup of tea brings deep refreshment. There is always nourishment in silence, whatever the depth.

This holds true even more so among friends. To walk, sit, eat in silence, aware of the other's presence is a communication of being. It is the experience of the other in their essence, before their becoming somebody. It can be as shocking as death, as astonishing as birth.

And there is a silence beyond silence, deeper still, with no sounds to compare it to. Here is the resting place of the Buddha Within.

31

BEAUTY

The Buddha said of the Dhamma that it was beautiful in the beginning, beautiful in the middle and beautiful in the end.

In the Parinibbana Discourse where the last of his days are recounted, we read that:

'Then the Blessed One, getting ready in the forenoon, took bowl and robe and went into Vesali for alms. After the alms round and meal, on his return, he spoke to the Venerable Ananda, saying: "Take up a mat, Ananda, and let us spend the day at the Capala shrine".'

Indeed, he rejoiced in the beauty of shrines: 'Delightful, Ananda, is Vesali; pleasant are the shrines of Udena, Gotamaka, Sattambaka, Bahuputta, Sarandada and Capala.'

In the early days, monastics would take pieces of leftover white cloth from the corpses in the charnel grounds and stitch them together. The Buddha must have thought order members looked scruffy in these because he asked them to cut and sew the pieces together so the robe when stretched out looked like paddy fields – and to dye them in areca nut which gave them a brownish hue.

All religions make great efforts to build beautiful places of worship and fill them with beautiful decorative art, statues and music.

But evil can also be beautiful. Mythologically, Lucifer was the most beautiful of angels. Leni Riefanstahl glorifies the Nazis in her propaganda films such as

The Triumph of the Will (1935). The martial parades of Communist Russia were a marvel to behold. The mushroom of an atomic bomb is beautiful.

Beauty then is a category of its own. Just because something is beautiful does not mean it is true or good.

How then do we experience beauty? It has a certain emotional feel that uplifts the heart. When we see a beautifully wrought iron gate or a dry-stone wall, we enter a pure aesthetic mental state. But more often than not something beautiful excites conjoining emotions of love, wonder, simple joy, devotion.

An eternal philosophical debate turns on whether beauty is in the eye of the beholder or out in the world. But in Buddhist understanding, it is the body-heart-mind complex that creates the world we experience.

So it is up to us. A mind full of beauty that highlights truth and virtue is a mental state we can presume the Buddha himself would delight in.

But if beauty or the beautiful feeling is our aim, then we have lost the path. Beauty has to be one of the many objectives that gather around our central aim to liberate ourselves from dukkha.

And external beauty is not necessary. We can liberate ourselves in a stinking slum, with raggedy clothes and only pap to eat.

32

DOWNERS

Depression was once less psychologised, not so medicalised. People talked of being under the weather. It was seen as part of life. We might be a bit down. We'd be told: 'Pull up your socks. Get on with it.' These downers are distinct from mental illness.

So long as we are feeling a bit depressed, the big problem is that we get miserable or angry or even anxious about it. That's what can drive 'a bit depressed' into a serious depression.

My first teacher was my mother. Today, she'd be considered to suffer a degree of clinical anxiety-driven depression. She ended up with a concoction of the pills so beloved of doctors. With new drugs on the market, she lived in an age when people started going to the GP with psychosomatic pain. She complained of low energy, an anxious stomach and headaches. Later in life, she told me that mothering her four children was what kept her going.

That was the first lesson: Just keep doing what you have to do – and do it with love.

My mother was sanguine with a slapstick type humour. She'd stick a needle in your bum while watching TV. And she transformed when she was with friends. No matter how she felt, she engaged and found happiness and fun in their company.

That was the second precious lesson: You've got to laugh!

I believe both strategies kept me from going under, but failed to tackle the root problem –my relationship to my 'downers'. Only when I began to meditate was I really able to grapple with them. The Buddha asks us to truly confront these feelings, not aggressively, but in a welcoming, kind, open-hearted way. He has a method for expressing this intimate embrace. He instructs us to 'feel feelings in feelings', to experience 'mental states in mental states'. In other words, no barriers caused by aversion or fear. For when we do not want to feel them, we seek distraction. Anything will do. Watch TV. Eat chocolate. And worse! If these poor strategies fail, then we truly begin to go under.

Much trust is needed to open up to these dark whirlpools. At times we may feel overwhelmed – that's when we need the teacher or therapist. But as we persist, we see we are creating a different relationship towards aching states of mind and harrowing emotions. This is one of radical acceptance: This is the way it is. Equanimity: Open-hearted, open-minded, no resistance, and patient forbearance. We experience a willingness to bear with mental pain. When we discover this new relationship of non-aggression and non-fear, something magical begins. All that oppressive turbulence is allowed to express itself fully and in so doing exhausts itself. Slowly these moods no longer hijack our lives. They become less dense and don't hang around so long.

Then it dawns that we've found the way not simply to end depression, but to end all suffering. This is the gift of Dhamma the Buddha gave to humanity – the understanding of how we create suffering for ourselves and how we can bring it all to an end.

33

MONEY AND POWER

When it comes to money and power, the Buddha, coming from a very different age, has only general guidelines for us today. For instance, here is a wise counsellor advising his king: 'Your majesty, the country is beset by thieves. It is ravaged; villages and towns are being destroyed ... If your majesty were to tax this region that would be the wrong thing to do. If your majesty [were] to get rid of this plague of robbers by executions and imprisonment ... the plague would not be ended properly. Those who survive would later harm the realm. However, this plan will eliminate the plague ... to [farmers] let your majesty distribute grain and fodder; to those in trade, capital; those in government service, a proper living wage.' DN5 (In the Buddha's Words by Bhikkhu Bodhi)

The Buddha's teaching spread through different eastern cultures and established medieval societies. With the onset of the industrial revolution, the tech revolution and modernism, even post-modernism, the Dhamma has yet to be fully adapted.

The combination of money and power can be lethal and the discrepancy between the one-percenters and high earners (including those who head charities!) and the lowest paid is undermining social cohesion. Some economists say this inequality is bad for the economy! As it is our civic duty to have a perspective on the financial, social and political landscape, how might we consider a change?

Christianity has been in the thick of change and heavily challenged. Within its various responses, perhaps distributism is closest to the Buddha's thinking.

This social doctrine, often described as a middle ground between capitalism and socialism, has deep roots in Catholic teachings. Based on the idea of equality, it is expressed in terms of subsidiarity and solidarity.

Subsidiarity, familiar to us as once EU members, originated in the Catholic Church. Politically, the Oxford English Dictionary defines it as 'the principle that a central authority should have a subsidiary function, performing only those tasks which cannot be performed at a more local level.' An example is where the local councils might take action rather than the government. Solidarity is unity or agreement of feeling or action, especially among individuals with a common interest, for example mutual support within a group, which is a core principle of trade unions.

The argument acknowledges the fallacy of giving ownership (that is, control) either to the boss (capitalism) or to the state (socialism). Distributism seeks to return ownership to everyone on the basis that the dispossessed would then have greater control and greater power in the local community (subsidiarity) and at higher levels of governments by forming pressure groups (solidarity).

Why ownership? Because the owner takes better care than the one who rents or works for. I've rented and I've bought a house; I've worked for someone and I have worked for myself; so to me the psychology of this is obvious.

For some Buddhists who think all possession is wrong this is a no-no. Or as Proudhon, the first to declare himself an anarchist, said: 'All property is theft!' That a monastic 'owns' their robes and bowl may come as a surprise. In fact, every time I get a new set of robes, I put a bindu (mark) on it to distinguish it as my own. A bit of 'all property is theft' was once afoot among monks with some making off with robes not their own. Since they didn't possess them, how could it be taking what is not freely given?

It's not what but how we possess that presents the problem, of course. When someone makes off with the mobile, we still go around saying someone stole 'my' mobile. But it's hardly 'mine' since the thief now has it. Possession of objects is a legal construct and can be an attachment. But when we realise that we can only use them, we free ourselves of stress and possessiveness. Just as monastics own their robes, so an individual can own his property, own her business.

As for solidarity, it is a core Sangha principle. To quote a well-known saying of the Buddha: Admirable friendship, admirable companionship, admirable camaraderie is actually the whole of the holy life. By which we can include all society. We are much more likely to build societal solidarity when we all feel we have something to cherish and defend – our property or business or community. Political jargon uses the word stakeholder.

Self-esteem is rooted in the ability to make, and take responsibility for, our own decisions and so have power over our life. This power can never be complete but the more of it we have, the greater our self-esteem, our respect for others – and our sense of responsibility.

So it is that power and riches feed one another for better or for worse.[18]

---

[18] You may be interested in this documentary about the Capitalist System. Four Horsemen – Feature Documentary – Official Version https://www.youtube.com/watch?v=5fbvquHSPJU

34

THE TREASURE OF THINGS

Every year we try to give away the stuff we've accumulated – things that we don't use now such as two pressure cookers or items people have left behind like scarves, shoe, even coats. If we can't give them away, we take them to a charity shop and if they won't have them, to recycling.

It is a practice I am developing to express gratitude to the object. I don't think the object is aware of my thankfulness. But that's really not the point. In our society where objects are so cheap, we discard them without a blink. It wasn't so in the poor 1950s in my childhood. A broken cup would deserve a severe reprimand and a reminder that 'cups cost money'.

Recognising the preciousness of our homes, clothes, pens, mobiles (without which we can no longer live!), develops an attitude of treasuring things. And that brings joy to the heart.

This treasuring of things assists our mindfulness. If everything is seen as a rare Ming vase, we will pick things up carefully, handle them carefully, put them down carefully. This is honouring the Buddha's last exhortation: 'Strive diligently.' And how can we possibly forget where we put the keys!

A problem may arise, however, with treasuring – and that is attachment. So it's good practice to remind ourselves that we can only use things. The idea of ownership is a psychological construct. The object does not feel owned. It can be used by a thief. It is a legal fiction necessary for an orderly society.

But how difficult it is to let go of something that has served us so well. I was bought a pair of boots at a cost of 40$! They were gloves to my feet, lasted years and then water began to seep in. I tried all sorts of ways to maintain them and each failed. Finally, I had to consign them to the wheelie bin. But not without a lingering fear I would never find such a pair of boots again.

Treasuring things also makes us tidy. Something I'm working on! Only in the rarest of cases do meditators fold the blanket neatly. It's just another one of those useless, time wasting things we have to do. But bringing gratitude to mind, recognising the work that has gone into making it, acknowledging it as a gift of nature and how it keeps us warm, we would naturally fold it carefully. And when we do things carefully, we naturally do them beautifully. And when we do things beautifully, joy arises naturally.

This is all part of our commitment to bring the Dhamma practice into everyday life.

35

HUMOUR IS A FUNNY THING

There are so many types of humour – some have listed twenty. But what inspires it?

Our delusion about who or why we are expresses itself as the opposite of the Three Existential Characteristics of Impermanence, Unsatisfactoriness and Not-self. Arising from the self there is a feeling of continuously being here and because it is driven by the desires to keep on becoming, there arise the attitudes of acquisitiveness, aversion and fear.

The purpose of humour is to see this folly, not by way of intellectual understanding, but by way of paradox. When this paradox is told humorously it makes us laugh but also relieves us of the wrong attitude.

The self does not really believe it is going to die. A man fell off a multi-storey office building. And as he passed each office they heard him say: So far so good!

But humour has its dark side when it arises out of aversion – this is sarcasm and sardonic satire. Unfortunately, it does make us laugh.

US President George Bush Junior was generally thought to be a little dim-witted and many false stories grew up around him.

On visiting an old people's home, he asked an elderly woman: 'Do you know who I am?' She replied: 'No, I don't. But I'm sure they'll tell you at the office.'

Politicians especially have to be thick skinned. But sarcasm can undermine relationships. After all it needs victims and it needs others to laugh at them.

And there is gallows humour, which eases the horror of a situation.

The great wit, Oscar Wilde, while dying in penury in a seedy Parisian hotel turned to the shabby wallpaper and supposedly said: 'My wallpaper and I are fighting a duel to the death. One or other of us has got to go.'

And what about slapstick and farce that expresses the sheer joy of living while showing our all too human foibles. We need only think of Charlie Chaplin (The Gold Rush), Jacques Tati (Mr Hulot's Holiday) and Peter Sellers (The Pink Panther), to bring a smile to your face. And it's warm smile.

The Buddha definitely enjoyed pulling a leg or two. Ajahn Sujato offers ten examples.
https://sujato.wordpress.com/2011/11/29/the-ten-funniest-scenes-from-the-pali-canon/

For example, Sujato records a particularly encounter with Dighanakha an obvious nickname meaning Long Nails and the Buddha. With great self-assurance he declares his understanding: 'Nothing is pleasing to me.' The Buddha's quickfire response: 'Well, this view of yours, is that pleasing to you?'

What makes us laugh tells us something about ourselves. Aware of our reactions to different types of humour from the cruelty of sarcasm to the playfulness of slapstick is a window onto our attitudes.

And our laughter? Is it choked? Hollow? Or open and hearty?

36

PURPOSE IN LIFE

'If you don't know where you are going, any road will take you there'. Lewis Carroll

In his inimitable quirky way, Lewis Carroll points to a profound truth about our lives: If we don't know where we're going not only do our lives lack central focus, they also have no meaning.

Without focus, aim or meaning, our lives drift – but not in any old haphazard way. We are already in any given moment conditioned beings. We have our habitual ways of understanding and acting on those understandings. And those understandings can be true – or false.

Our history is littered with 'ideologies', secular and religious, that have taken us down dark roads.

The Buddha's own avowed aim when he took up his mission to teach others to liberate themselves was to elucidate a path: a development and an aim. And most important, an understanding not based on philosophical abstraction, but based on his personal direct experience of his own progress and attainment.

Our idea of time as linear, an arrow that moves from past to present to future, lends itself to a view of progress that presumes from worse we getter better, and from better we get even better (for the pessimist it is the opposite).

We may consider this to be true when we think of science which investigates the physical and psychological worlds with a view to understand and then, as is our nature, to control them. This has led to a technology that astonishes. Yet it is common observation that when it comes to ethics, comparable progress is not evident in how we as humans relate to each other, to other living beings and nature. Indeed, one might argue that it has all got worse.

While we can point to individual paragons of human goodness in the religious and secular life, they remain a rarity and always arise as a response to general unethical behaviour, such as apartheid, regime oppression and careless destruction of our environment. And there are legions, yes legions, of people involved in putting the world to rights whether the focus be climate crisis, slavery or political oppression to mention some of the worst.

How then would progress manifest in a world truly devoted to Dhamma? Because our aim is to achieve liberation from suffering, we look into the causes of that suffering. We find its root to be selfishness. It's really all about me! When we realise this 'me' is a mistaken understanding of how we really are, we begin to change.

Before we thought 'me' was independent, a self-willed integer, complete and entire unto 'myself'. On careful observation and reflection, we begin to realise this 'me' is entirely dependent on my relationship with other beings and the surrounding world. I am inextricably bound up in the total environs that envelope me. I cannot exist outside this milieu.

This invites us to develop those attitudes that will lead the whole environment towards harmony since in harmony we find our peace and joy.

In that harmony people are more than willing to support each other in their spiritual quest. How easy it is to practise when surrounded by like-minded others on retreat. Or indeed, how joyful is the practice of affectionate mindfulness when doing something with others who have a similar goal.

So it helps to know where we are bound, no matter how nebulous the goal. The Buddha says our ultimate goal is Nibbana. But what can that be? Rather than fretting over something that is by definition beyond description, we can ground ourselves in the ethics manifested in how an Arahant, one who has attained Nibbana, lives. Then that path becomes clear. In short, the second step of the Eightfold Noble Path, Right Attitude, shows us where we are going – moving from selfishness to generosity, hatred to love and cruelty to compassion.

These social virtues cannot be practised on 'me'. They demand the 'other'. And in that relationship, the 'other' is encouraged to reciprocate as we are encouraged when the 'other' behaves towards us with generosity, love and compassion.

It would be delusive to believe we would end up in Shangri-La, for this is Samsara after all. But we may move from a disharmonious social order based on competition to one based on harmonious co-operation.

SATIPANYA BUDDHIST RETREAT

Satipanya Buddhist Retreat is informally affiliated to a group of meditation centres in Sri Lanka. The order is the Swejjin Chapter within the Amarapura Nikaya (order). This is the Monastic Sangha that Bhante Bodhidhamma belongs to.

Buddhism has come to the West in all its varied forms. Satipanya follows the meditation system developed by the Venerable Mahasi Sayadaw of Burma. It is hoped that Satipanya offers a clear vision so that retreatants can decide whether this is the form best suited for them.

There are many Mahasi centres and groups within UK and Europe. www.Mahasi.EU is a twin site for **Mahasi** meditation in North America(Canada & USA): **www.mahasi**.US

Satipanya welcomes all, irrespective of ethnicity, gender, sexual orientation, disability, political persuasion and, most important, religious persuasion.

Mahasi Vipassana Insight Meditation:

Our insight meditation (vipassana) is grounded in the tradition of the Burmese meditation master, Mahasi Sayadaw, who began to teach vipassana insight meditation after World War II near Yangon (Rangoon) in Myanmar (Burma).

He developed a method to help us maintain moment to moment mindfulness from the instant we awake to the instant we fall asleep. There are two techniques: the use a simple word to note whatever we are experiencing and doing everything very slowly. Silence is maintained the whole while.

This leads not only to spiritual insights into our true, unborn-undying essence, but also, equally important, to the purification of the heart. So that we not only become wiser but more caring, generous, joyous and compassionate.

We follow a robust schedule, but meditators can modulate their practice to fit their level of experience, even absolute beginners. The accent is on relaxation and curiosity, rather than striving and concentration. And regular teacher contact, daily Q&A and personal interviews ensures students are supported throughout.

The retreat ends with Metta (see below) and advice on how to bring the practice into ordinary daily life to enhance our relationships and give spiritual meaning to our work and everyday tasks.

Please note, experience is not necessary and remember you can often stay for one, two or more weeks.

Bhante Bodhidhamma began his Buddhist practice in the Soto Zen tradition at a monastery in the north of England, Throssel Hole Priory. He was living in Birmingham at the time and through his teacher, Vajira Bailey, was introduced to Ven.Dr.Rewata Dhamma, a Burmese monk who established the Birmingham Buddhist Centre and Peace Pagoda. Out of interest he began to practise vipassana, with the then abbot, Ajhan Sumedho, of Cittaviveka, the Thai Forest Sangha Monastery. About that time, the Mahasi Sayadaw came to England. He attended a course given by Sayadaw U Janaka, the teacher who accompanied him. In '82, he went to work with Sayadaw in Burma. Before long he wanted to spend more time in meditation and so ordained in '86. He spent the first years in England and then went to Sri Lanka. He joined an order of monks there who take their ordination from the Mahasi Sayadaw. He stayed at their main meditation centre at Kanduboda for eight years. He returned to England in '98 and began teaching. From 2001- 5, he was the resident teacher at Gaia House, a large meditation centre in the south of England which he acknowledges as his Dhamma Teacher Training College. During that time, he began with the help of supporters to establish the Satipanya Buddhist Trust, a registered charity (no. 1116668). The objective was to set up a small meditation centre dedicated to the Mahasi tradition. This aspiration was realised on April 2nd 2007, when Satipanya Buddhist Retreat was opened on the borders of Wales and England.

Satipanya
Buddhist Retreat

Satipanya is devoted
to the practice of insight meditation, Vipassana,
and the development of Contemplative Living.

If you have benefited from this book and wish to support our work, please send your donation to the address below.
Or access our website and donate on line..
We depend entirely on voluntary support.

Satipanya Buddhist Retreat
White Grit   Minsterley   Shropshire   SY5 0JN
Tel: 0044 (0)1588 650752   info: info@satipanya.org.uk
www.satipanya.org.uk

Printed in Great Britain
by Amazon